CASE UNSOLVED FILES

CASE No. 001 NORJAK

This book is dedicated to the men & women who have worked this case.

Photograph credits: Pages 92 and 93 (top): AP Images;
Pages 93 (bottom) and 94: Getty Images.

The illustration on p. 83 is based on the cover of
Dan Cooper - L'Affaire Minos. Reproduced with permission.

Balzer + Bray is an imprint of HarperCollins Publishers.
HarperAlley is an imprint of HarperCollins Publishers.

Unsolved Case Files: Escape at 10,000 Feet: D.B. Cooper and the Missing Money

For information address HarperCollins Children's Books, a division of HarperCollins Publishers, 195 Broadway, New York, NY 10007.
www.harperalley.com

Library of Congress Control Number: 2020941228
ISBN 978-0-06-299152-2 — ISBN 978-0-06-299151-5 (pbk.)

The artist used pens, pencils, and Adobe Photoshop to create the illustrations for this book. Typography by Tom Sullivan and Dana Fritts.
20 21 22 23 24 GPS 10 9 8 7 6 5 4 3 2 1
❖
First Edition

UNSOLVED CASE FILES

ESCAPE
AT 10,000 FEET

D.B. Cooper and the Missing Money

by TOM SULLIVAN

BALZER + BRAY

Imprints of HarperCollins*Publishers*

HARPER
alley

THIS IS A TRUE STORY.

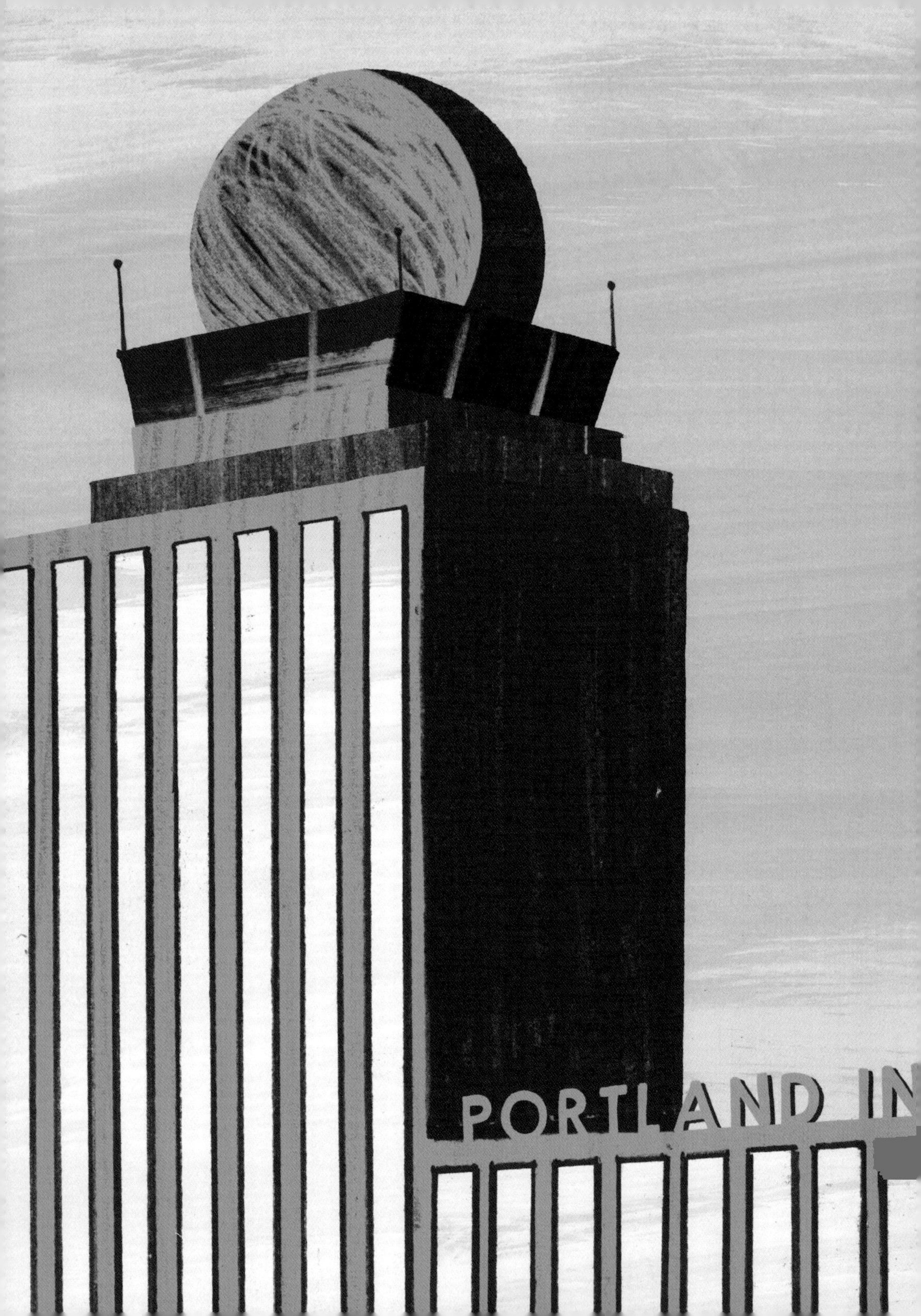
PORTLAND IN

PART ONE:

A MAN WITH A BRIEFCASE

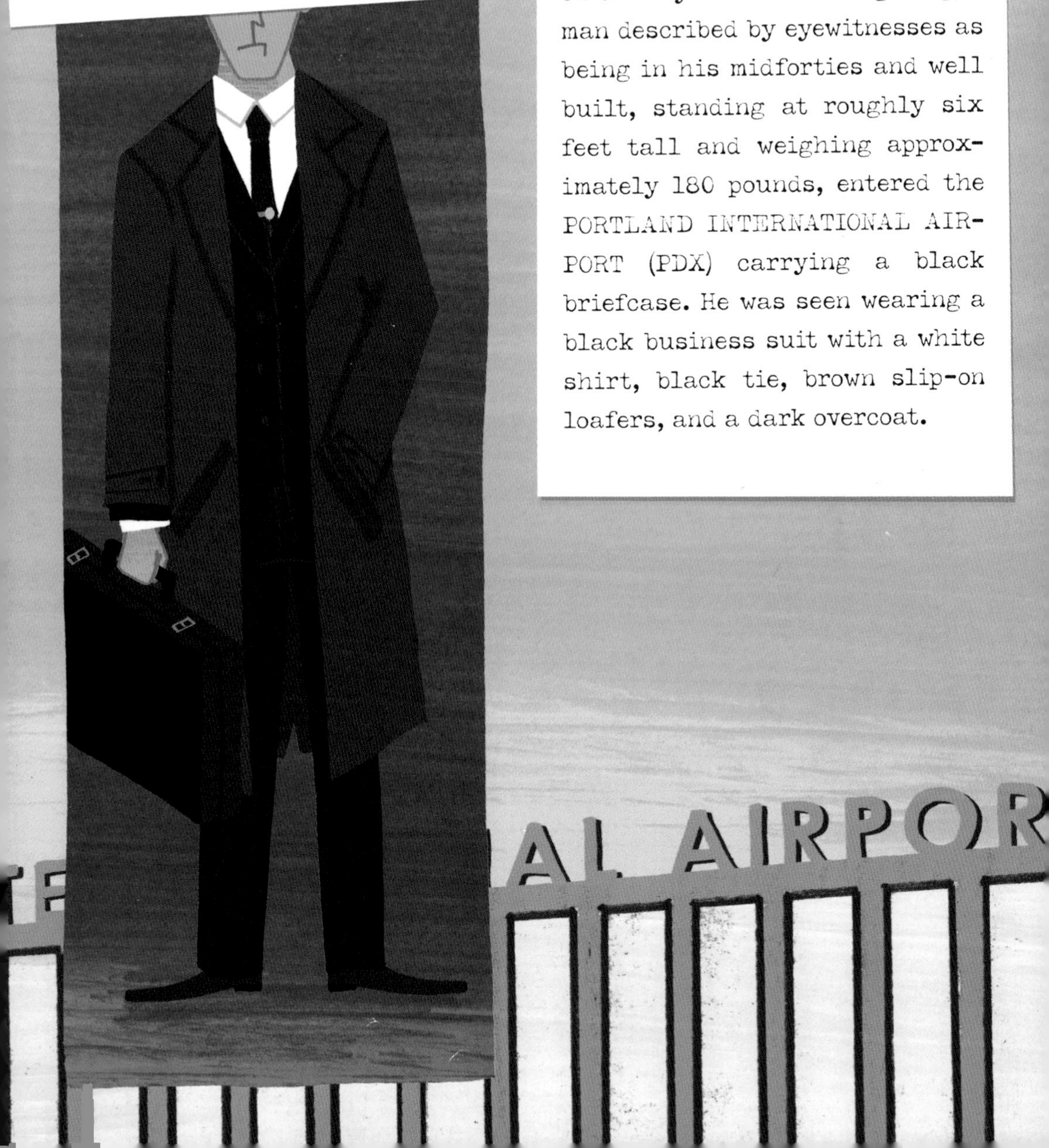

AL AIRPOR

NOVEMBER 24, 1971
PORTLAND, OREGON

2:00 p.m.

On the day before Thanksgiving, a man described by eyewitnesses as being in his midforties and well built, standing at roughly six feet tall and weighing approximately 180 pounds, entered the PORTLAND INTERNATIONAL AIRPORT (PDX) carrying a black briefcase. He was seen wearing a black business suit with a white shirt, black tie, brown slip-on loafers, and a dark overcoat.

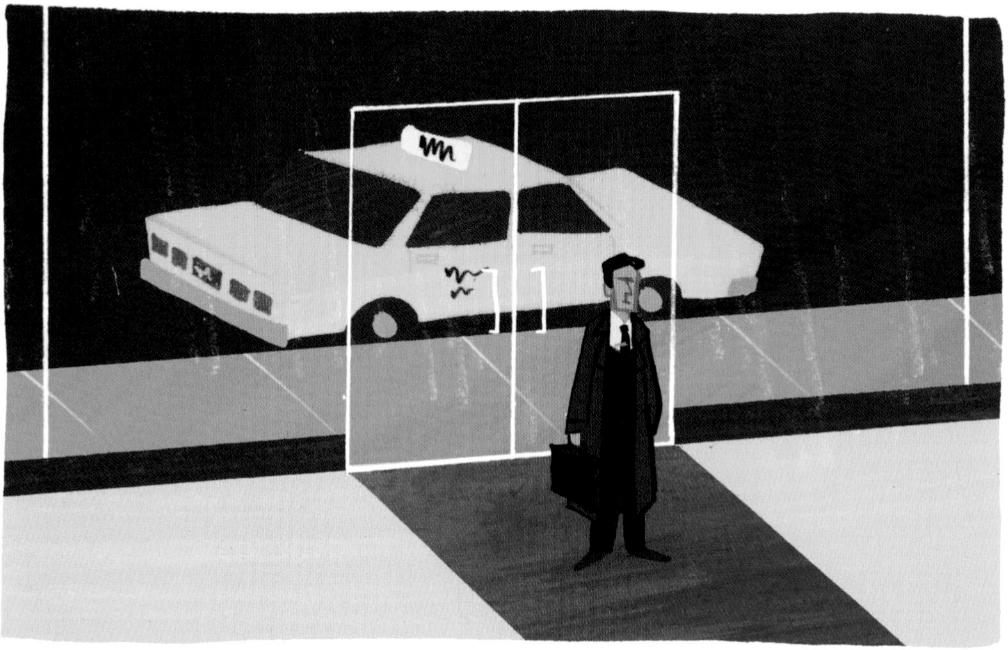

Once inside the terminal, the man approached the ticket counter for NORTHWEST ORIENT AIRLINES.

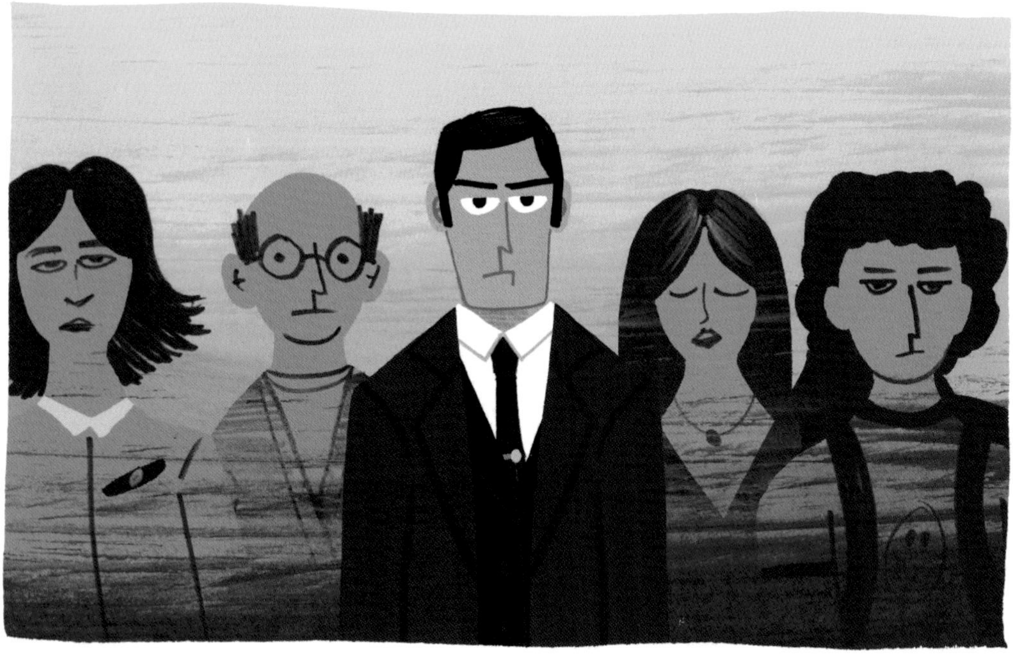

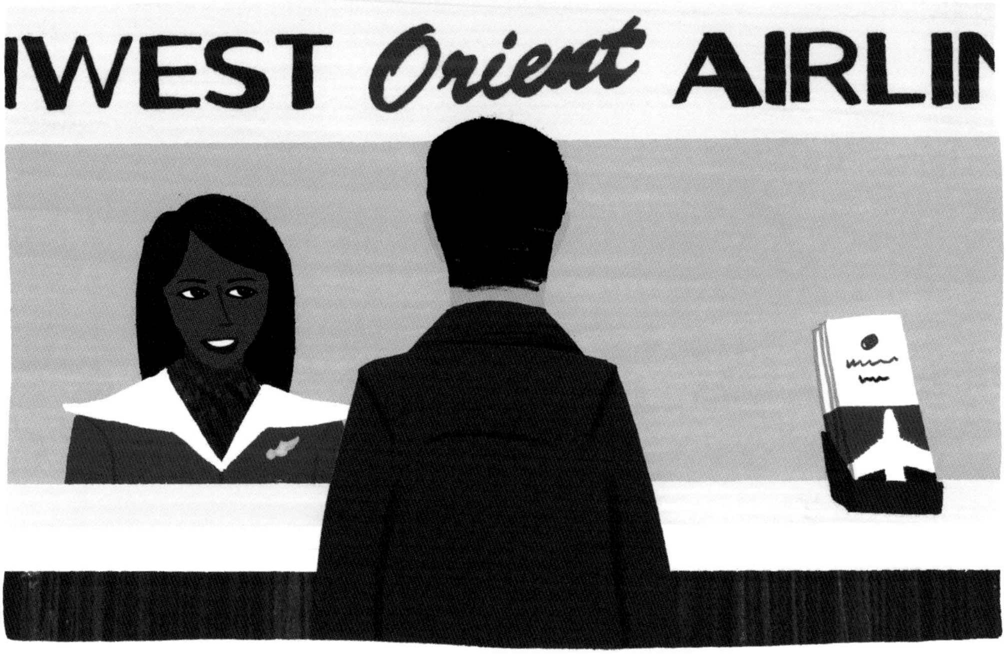
IWEST Orient AIRLI

Identifying himself as DAN COOPER, he purchased a one-way ticket to SEATTLE, WASHINGTON, on flight number 305 with $20 cash.

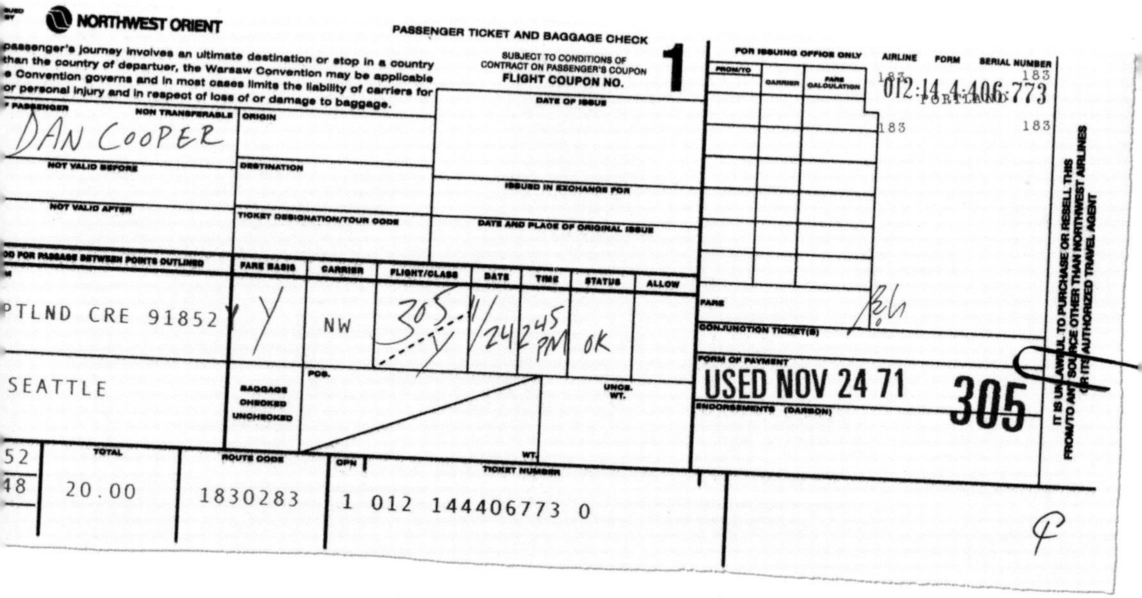

NORTHWEST ORIENT

PASSENGER TICKET AND BAGGAGE CHECK

SUBJECT TO CONDITIONS OF CONTRACT ON PASSENGER'S COUPON

FLIGHT COUPON NO. 1

passenger's journey involves an ultimate destination or stop in a country than the country of departuer, the Warsaw Convention may be applicable e Convention governs and in most cases limits the liability of carriers for or personal injury and in respect of loss of or damage to baggage.

PASSENGER — NON TRANSFERABLE: DAN COOPER

ORIGIN / DESTINATION / DATE OF ISSUE / NOT VALID BEFORE / NOT VALID AFTER / ISSUED IN EXCHANGE FOR / TICKET DESIGNATION/TOUR CODE / DATE AND PLACE OF ORIGINAL ISSUE

FOR ISSUING OFFICE ONLY

AIRLINE FORM SERIAL NUMBER: 183 012:14 4:406:773 183 PORTLAND 183 183

GOOD FOR PASSAGE BETWEEN POINTS OUTLINED	FARE BASIS	CARRIER	FLIGHT/CLASS	DATE	TIME	STATUS	ALLOW
PTLND CRE 91852 Y	Y	NW	305 Y	11/24	2:45 PM	OK	
SEATTLE	BAGGAGE CHECKED UNCHECKED						

FARE — CONJUNCTION TICKET(S) — FORM OF PAYMENT: USED NOV 24 71 305

ENDORSEMENTS (CARBON)

TOTAL: 20.00 — ROUTE CODE: 1830283 — CPN / TICKET NUMBER: 1 012 144406773 0

IT IS UNLAWFUL TO PURCHASE OR RESELL THIS FROM/TO ANY SOURCE OTHER THAN NORTHWEST AIRLINES OR ITS AUTHORIZED TRAVEL AGENT

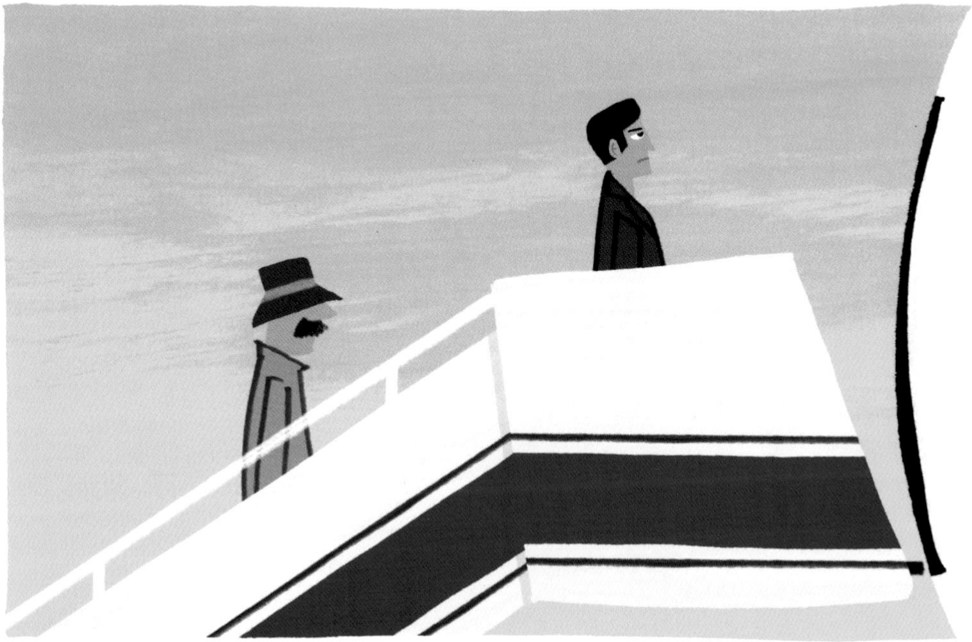

After boarding the plane second to last, COOPER made his way past the other thirty-five passengers currently on board and took his seat, 18-E, in the back row.

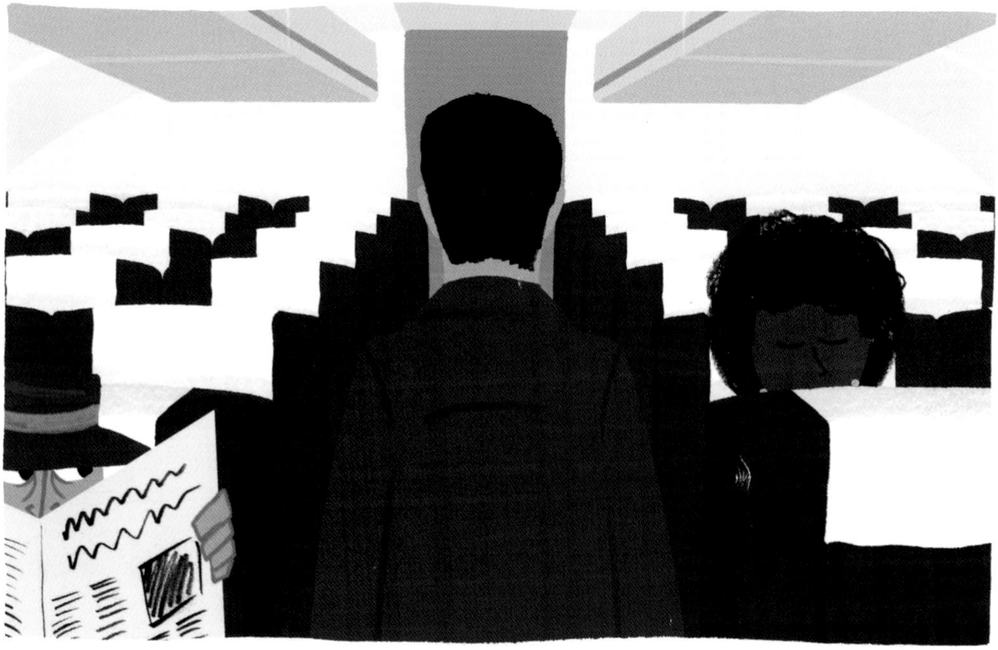

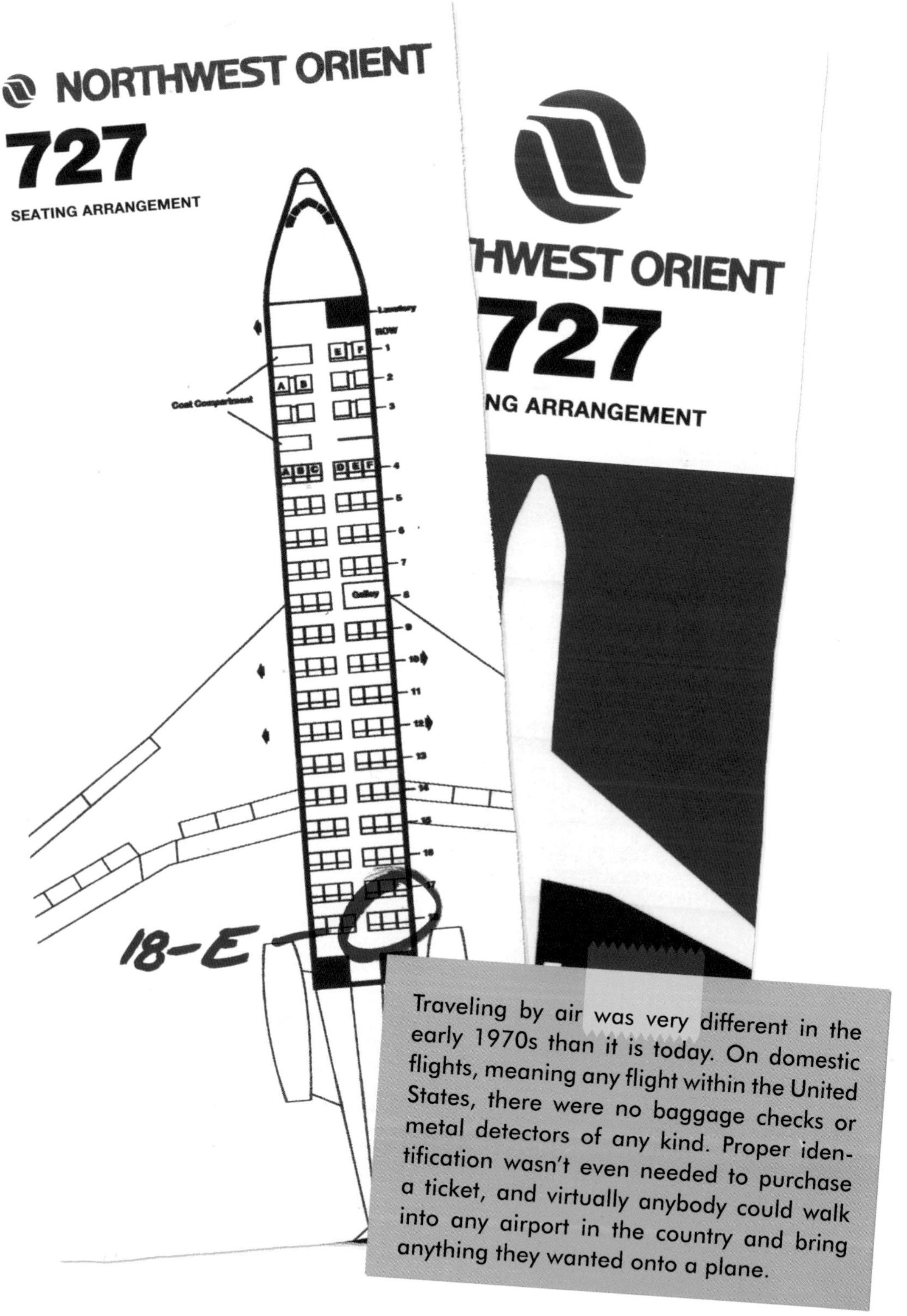
NORTHWEST ORIENT
727
SEATING ARRANGEMENT
Lavatory
ROW
Coat Compartment
Galley
18-E
THWEST ORIENT
727
NG ARRANGEMENT

Traveling by air was very different in the early 1970s than it is today. On domestic flights, meaning any flight within the United States, there were no baggage checks or metal detectors of any kind. Proper identification wasn't even needed to purchase a ticket, and virtually anybody could walk into any airport in the country and bring anything they wanted onto a plane.

Once seated, COOPER lit a cigarette, ordered a drink, and passed a note to flight attendant FLORENCE SCHAFFNER.

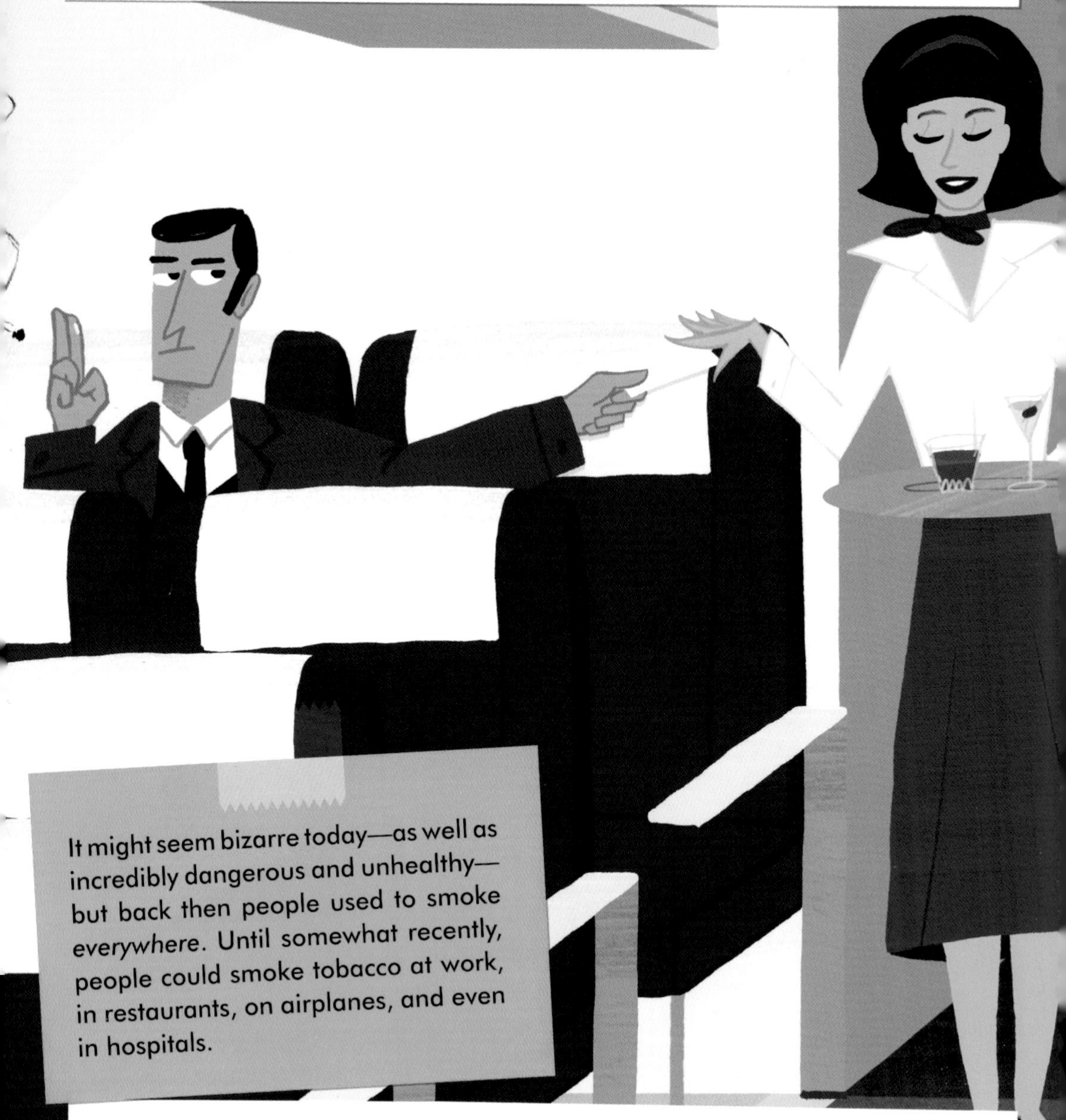

It might seem bizarre today—as well as incredibly dangerous and unhealthy—but back then people used to smoke everywhere. Until somewhat recently, people could smoke tobacco at work, in restaurants, on airplanes, and even in hospitals.

Assuming this was just another lonely businessman trying to ask her out on a date, Ms. SCHAFFNER slipped the note into her pocket without giving it much thought.

But upon the man's insistence, she unfolded the piece of paper.

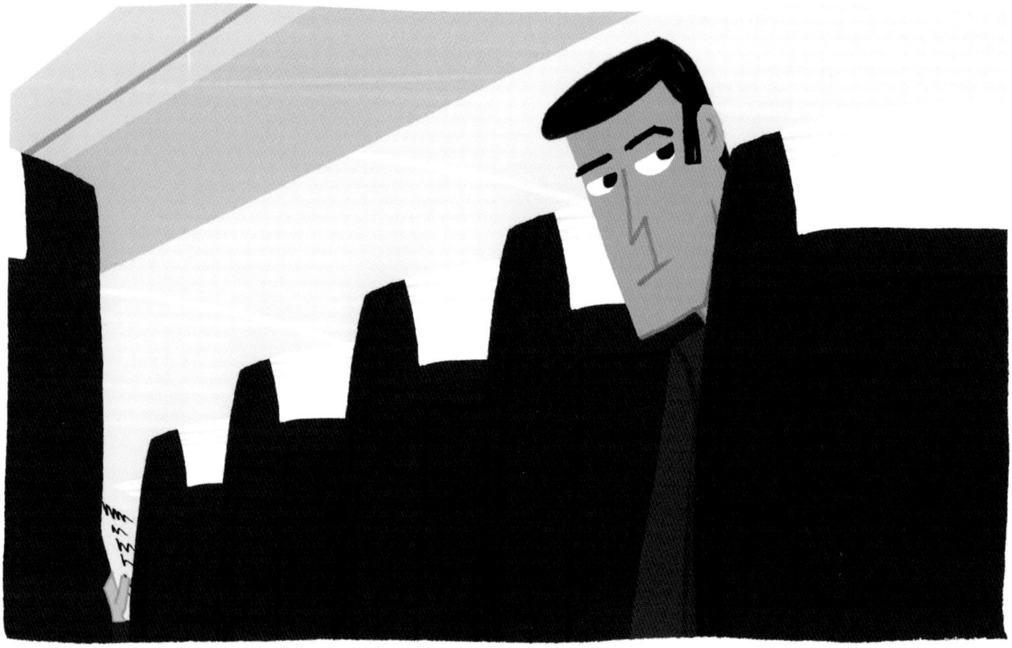

Written in black felt-tip pen were the words:

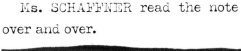

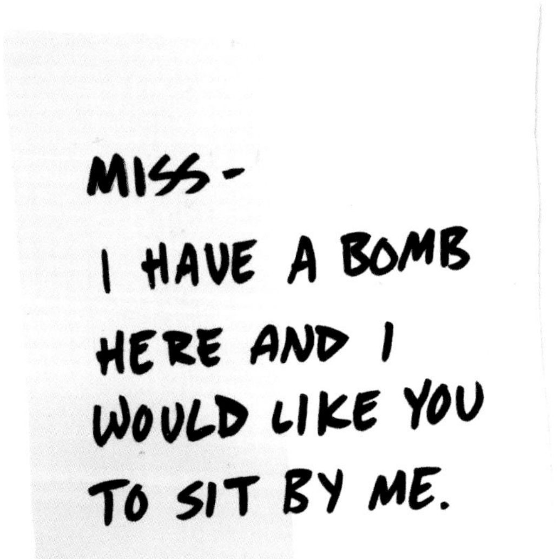
MISS-
I HAVE A BOMB
HERE AND I
WOULD LIKE YOU
TO SIT BY ME.

Ms. SCHAFFNER read the note over and over.

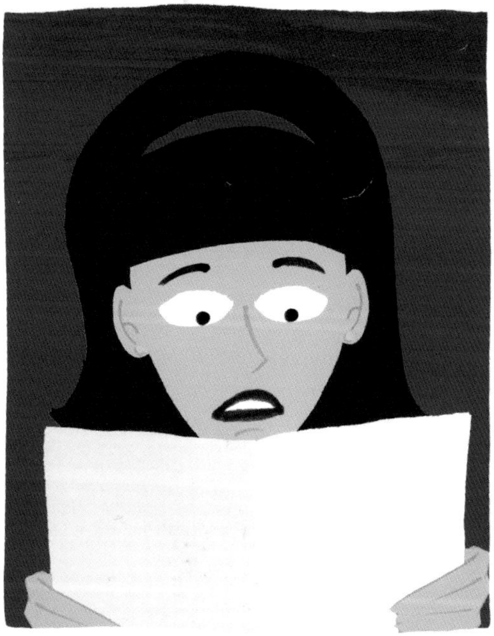

She asked the man if he was joking, but in a calm and serious tone, COOPER responded, "No, miss, this is for real."

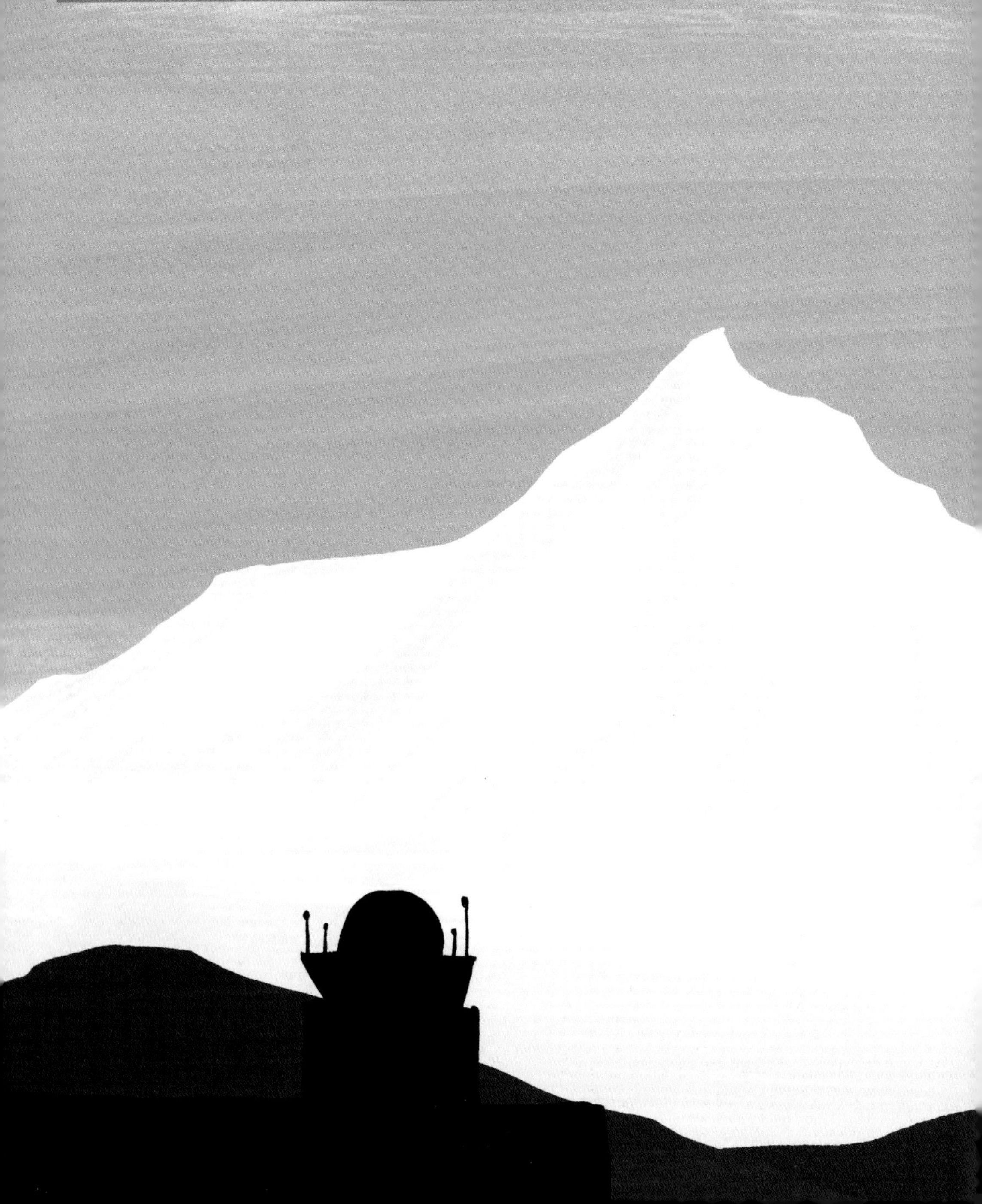

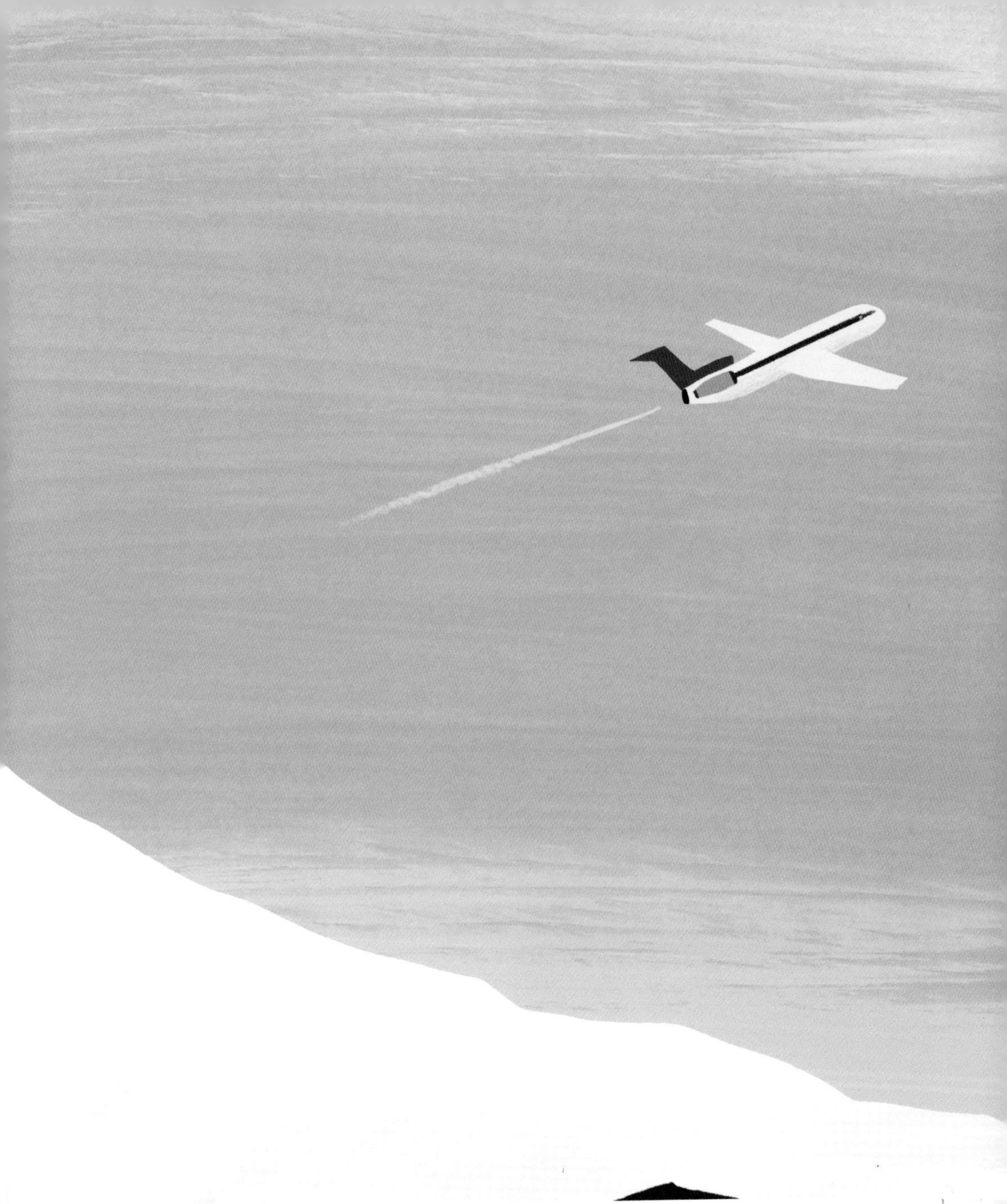

3:07 p.m.

Flight 305 reports wheels up at PDX bound for SEATTLE-TACOMA INTERNATIONAL AIRPORT (SEA).

Shortly after takeoff, flight attendant TINA MUCKLOW approached the back of the plane, and Ms. SCHAFFNER showed her the note.

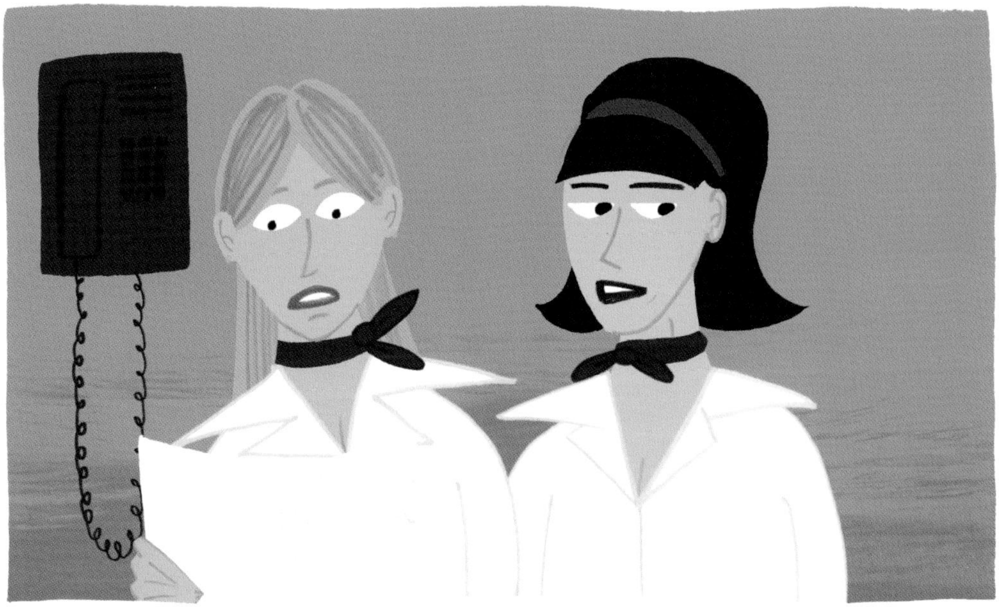

It was at this time that the hijacker put on a pair of dark-rimmed wraparound sunglasses in an effort to conceal his identity, and Ms. MUCKLOW picked up the intercom to relay to the pilot what was happening.

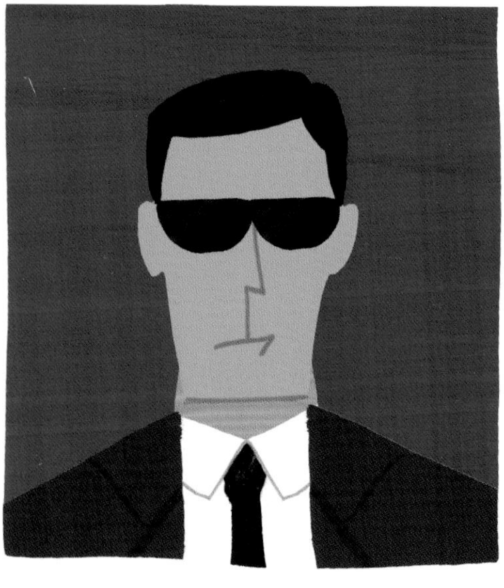

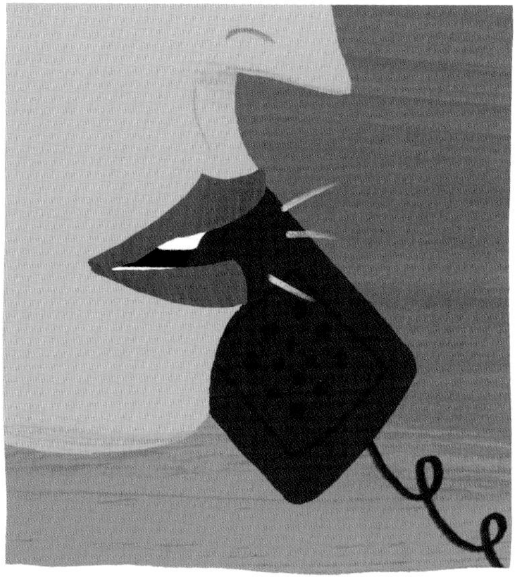

Meanwhile, a terrified Ms. SCHAFFNER sat down next to COOPER as instructed.

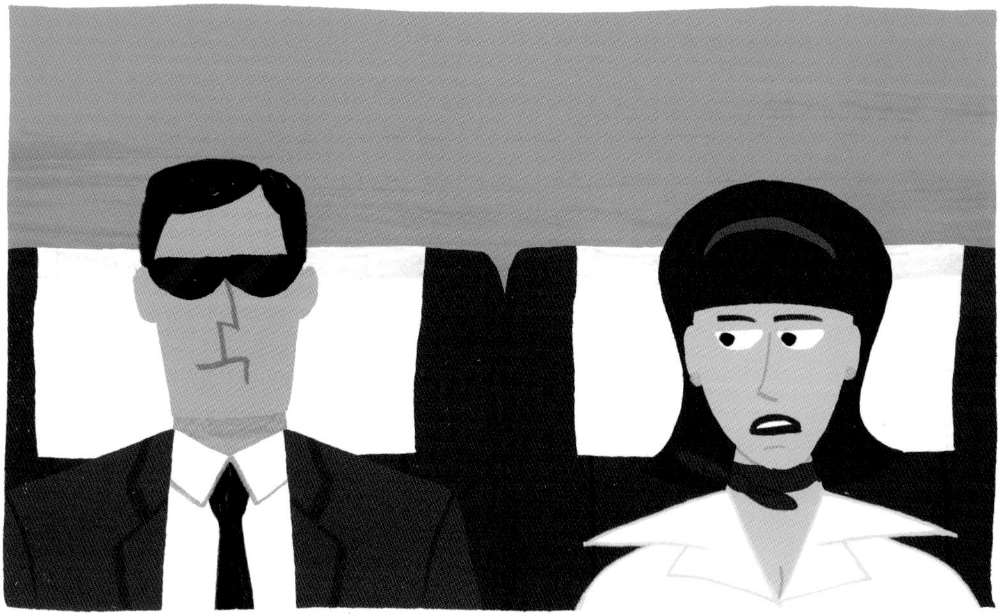

He opened his briefcase to reveal eight reddish sticks of what appeared to be dynamite that were bundled together with tape and wired to a battery. Holding a loose wire, COOPER indicated that he could detonate the device at any time.

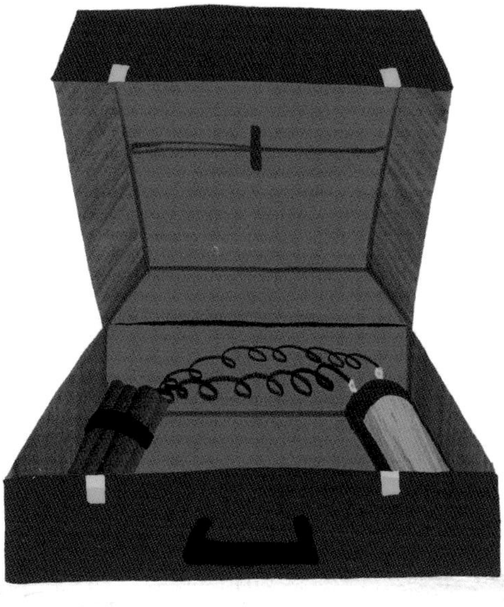

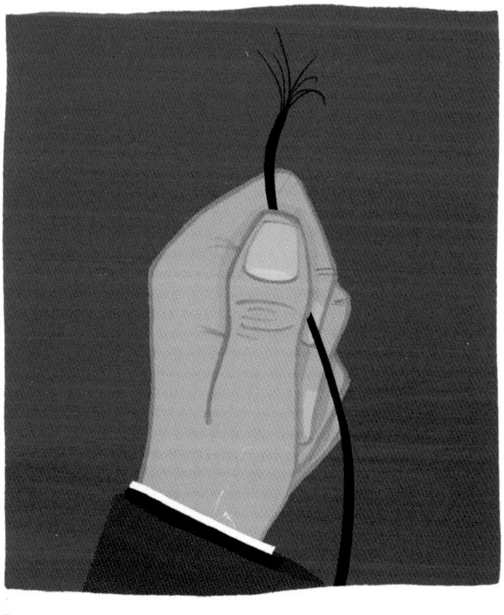

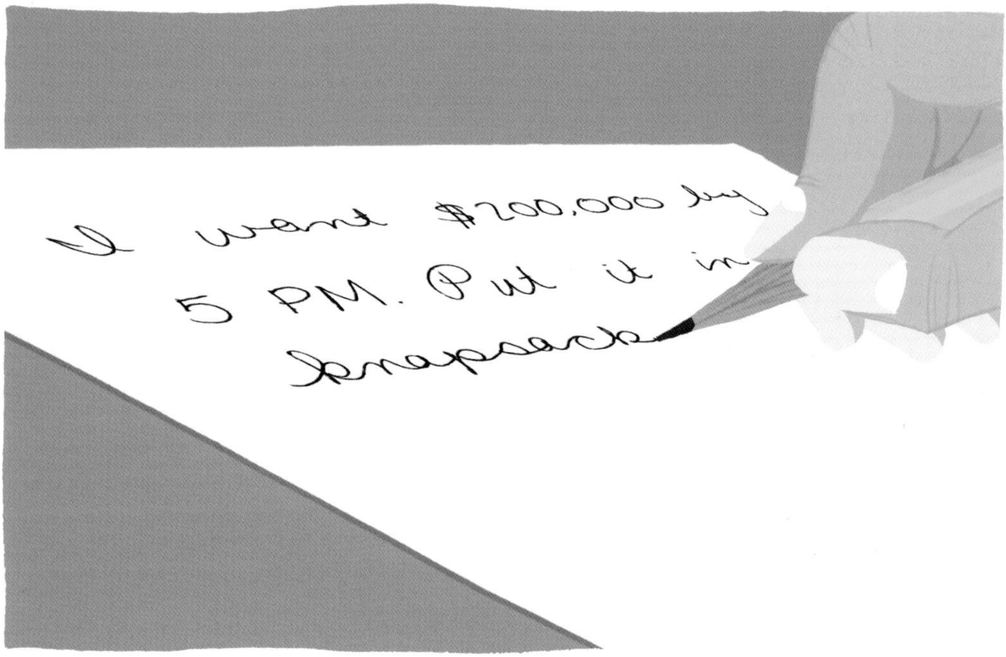
I want $200,000 by
5 PM. Put it in
knapsack

The hijacker then told Ms. SCHAFFNER to write down his list of demands and to deliver them to the captain.

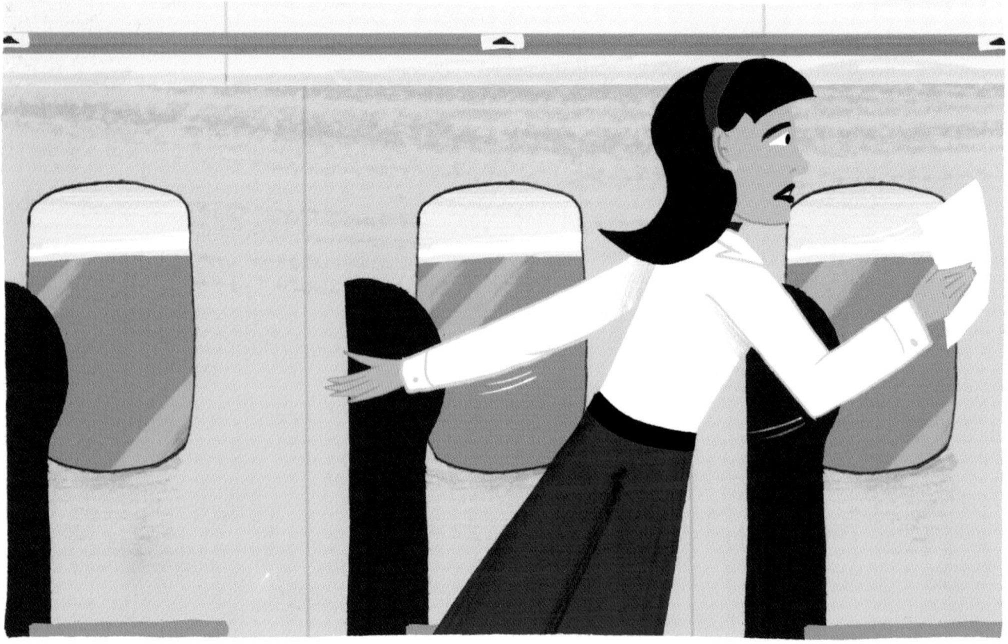

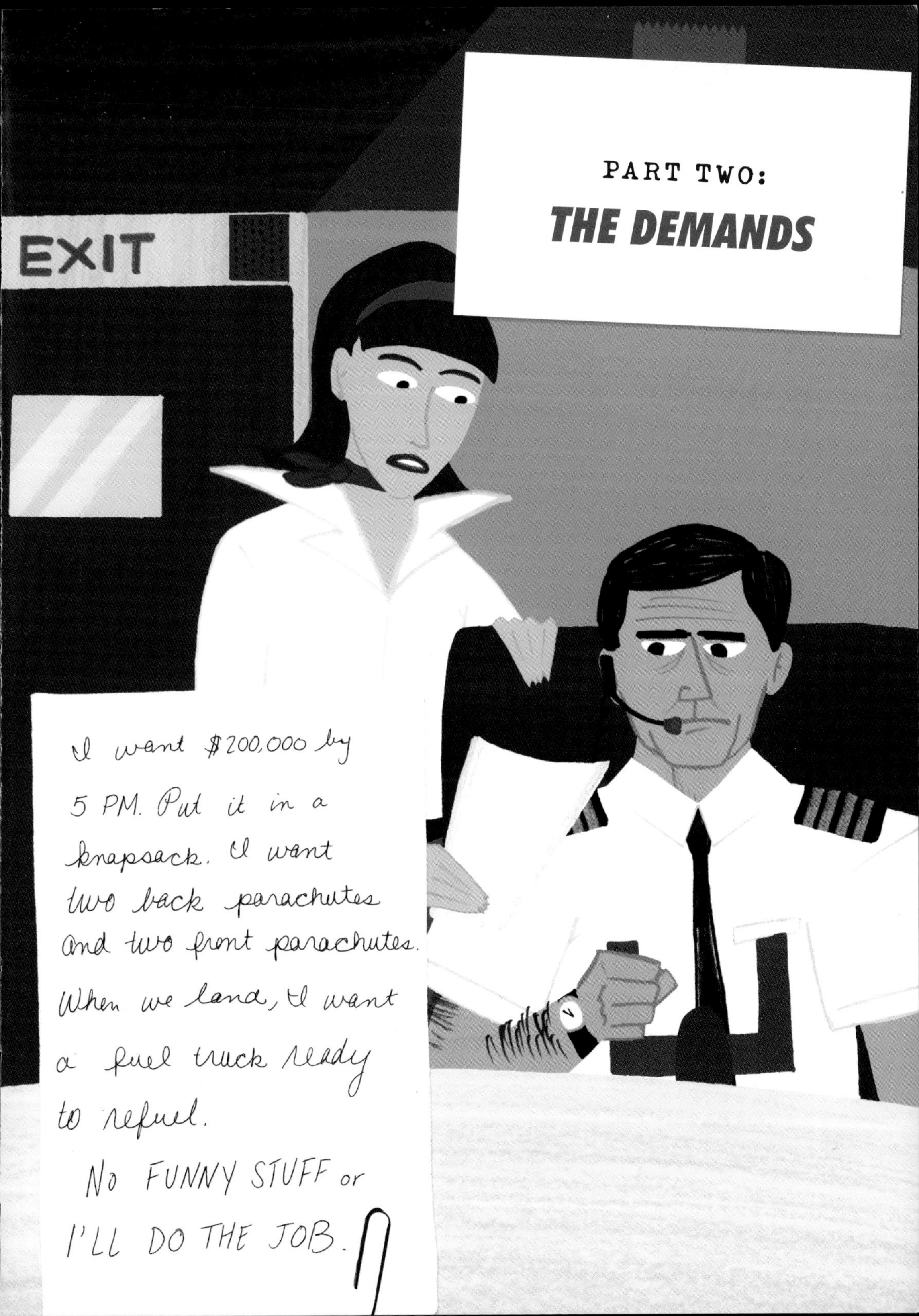
PART TWO:
THE DEMANDS
EXIT
I want $200,000 by 5 PM. Put it in a knapsack. I want two back parachutes and two front parachutes. When we land, I want a fuel truck ready to refuel.
No FUNNY STUFF or I'LL DO THE JOB.

3:13 p.m.

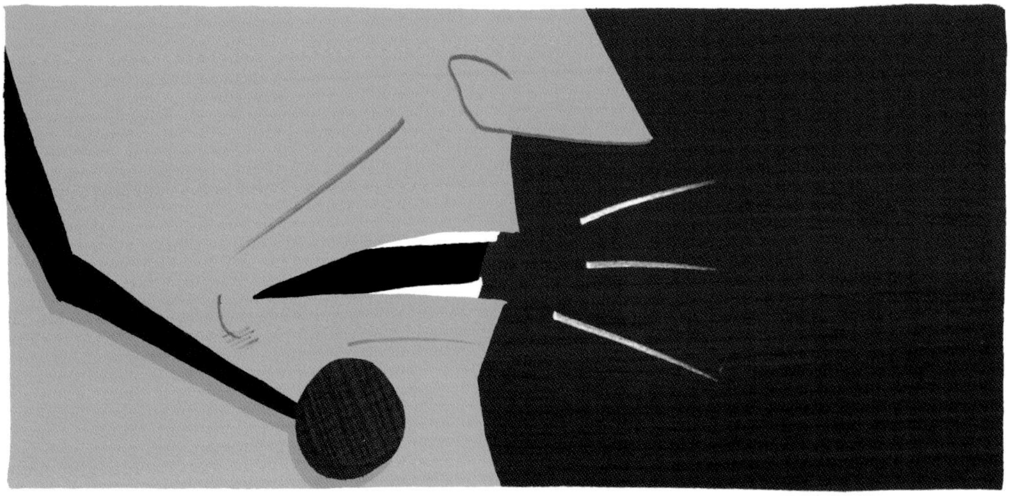

Captain WILLIAM SCOTT told Ms. SCHAFFNER to stay in the cockpit for the remainder of the flight. He then radioed Seattle-Tacoma air traffic control:

"Passenger is advising he is hijacking. En route to SEA. The stewardess has been handed a note requesting $200,000 and a knapsack by 5:00 p.m. this afternoon. He wants two backpack parachutes and two front parachutes. He wants the money in negotiable American currency. Denomination of the bills is not important. He has a bomb in his briefcase and will use it if anything is done to block his request. En route to SEA."

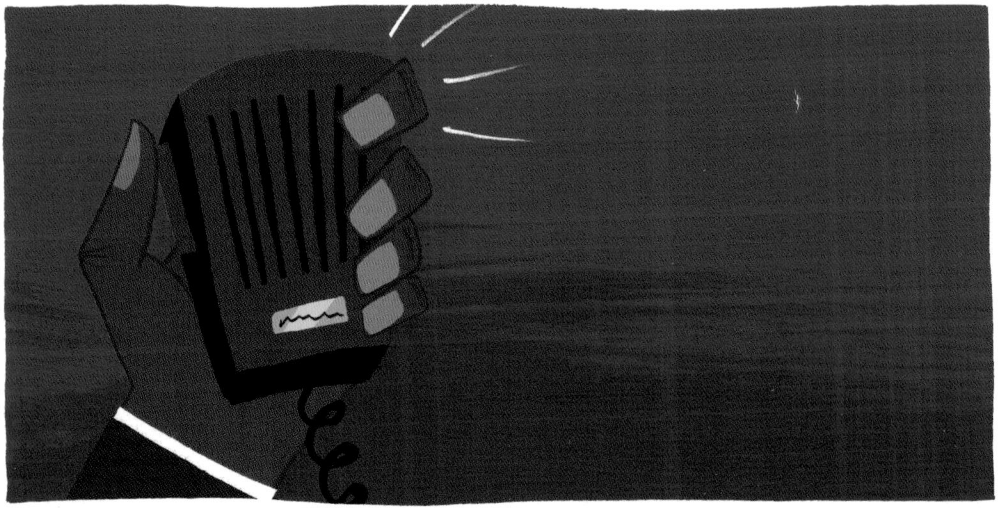

```
              11/24  ⊙↓
              305 OUT PDX 2253/2258 ETA SEA 2336 18.5
              RB
3:07 PM,  PST  KC2307CK



              11/24  ⊙↓
              305 PSGR ADV IS HIHAKING   ENRTE TO EA
              STEW HAS BEEN HANDED NOTE REQST  2HND   THSD
              AND KNAPSACK BY 5PM SEA   THIS AFTNN
              WANST  2 BAK PAK PARACHUTES
              WANTS MONEY IN NEGOTBL AMERICAN CURRNCY
              DENONMINATION OF BILLS NOT IMPORATANT
              HAS BOMB IN BRIEF CASE  AND ILL USE IT IF
              ANYTHING IS DONE TO BLOCK HI REQUEST
              ENRTE TO SEA
3:13 PM,  PST  KC2313CK



              1124 11/24  ⊙↓
              305 AFTR LANDG IN SEA   REQ NO  ONE MEET
              ACFT TO HINDER   DO NOT WANT ANY FBI
              AGENTS  OR ANYONE TO  EET ACFT
              WILL PARK ACFT OTHER THAN GATE  DO NOT
              WANT ANYONE TO  PRCH CFT FROM ANY DIRECTNS
               WIL ADV LATER INSTRCTNS  DO NOT WANT ANY
              EQUIP AT ACFT
              R
3:15 PM,  PST  KC2315CK



              11/24  ⊙↓
              305  ADV THE
              BRDD AT PDX
3:20 PM,  PST  MSPXR 2320CK
```

Back then, flight transcripts were recorded using a teletypewriter (TTY), which was a device that could send and receive printed messages. But the messages were usually abbreviated because they were transcribed in real time, and since there was no delete button, they were often riddled with spelling errors.

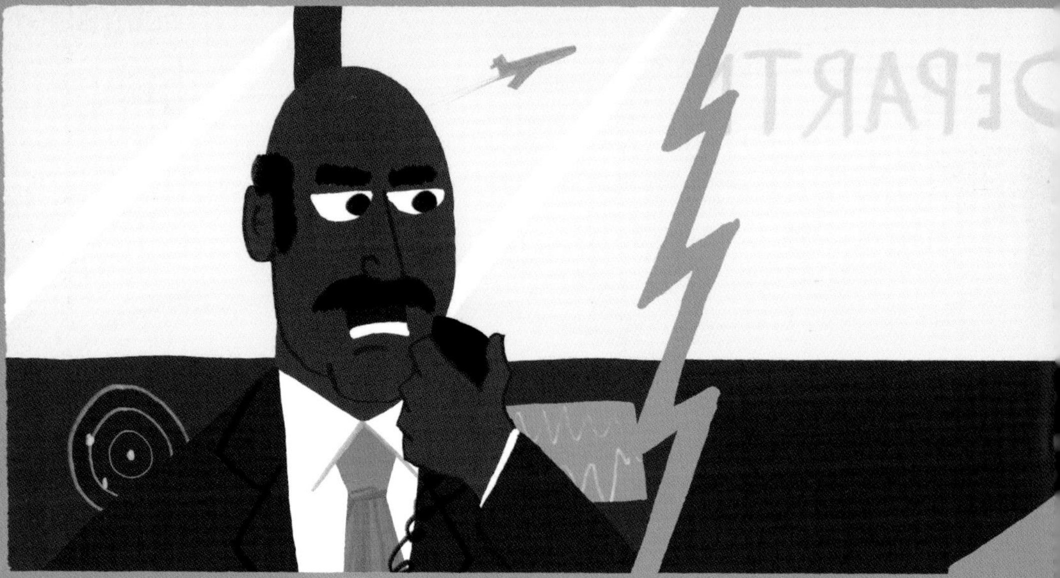

Air traffic control alerted the Seattle Police Department, who then notified the FBI.

Federal agents placed a call to Northwest Orient's president, DONALD NYROP, who, concerned with the safety of his passengers and crew, told the FBI to comply with the hijacker's demands.

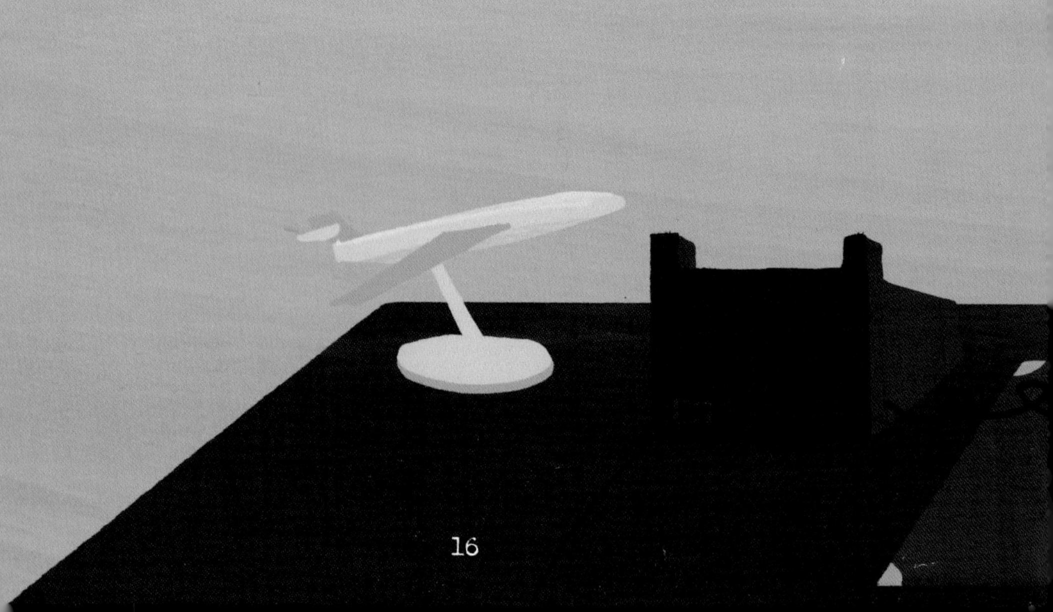

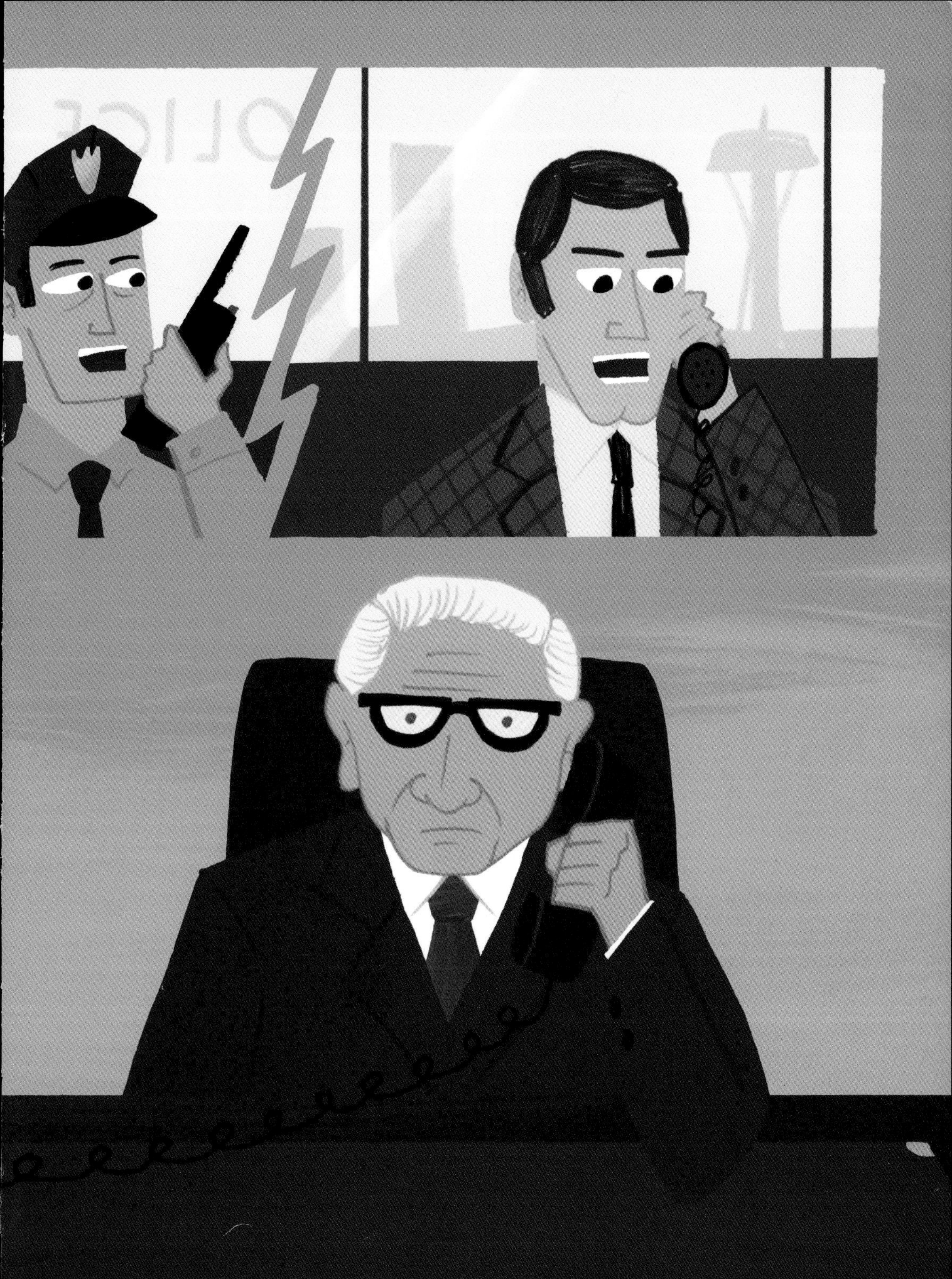

Typically the flight from Portland, Oregon, to Seattle, Washington, is a quick thirty-minute trip, but the authorities needed more than a half hour to meet the hijacker's demands, and COOPER was adamant that the plane not land until all his stipulations had been met.

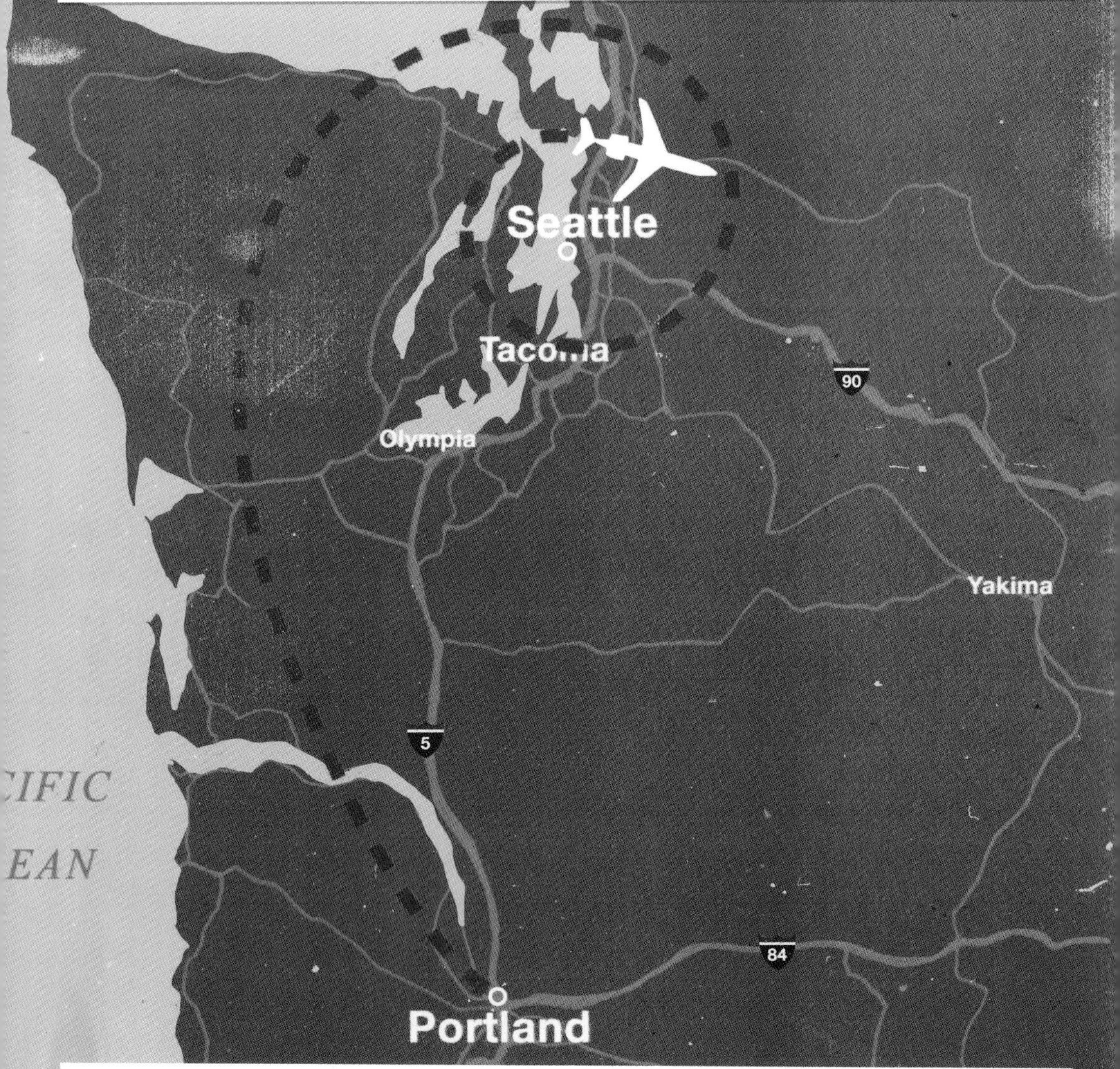
Seattle
90
Olympia
Yakima
5
84
Portland

Additionally, COOPER did not want the passengers on the plane to panic, or to even know that they were being hijacked, so the pilot told everyone that there was a mechanical issue with the plane and that they would need to burn off excess fuel before landing. The only way the flight crew could buy time was to circle in the air over Seattle.

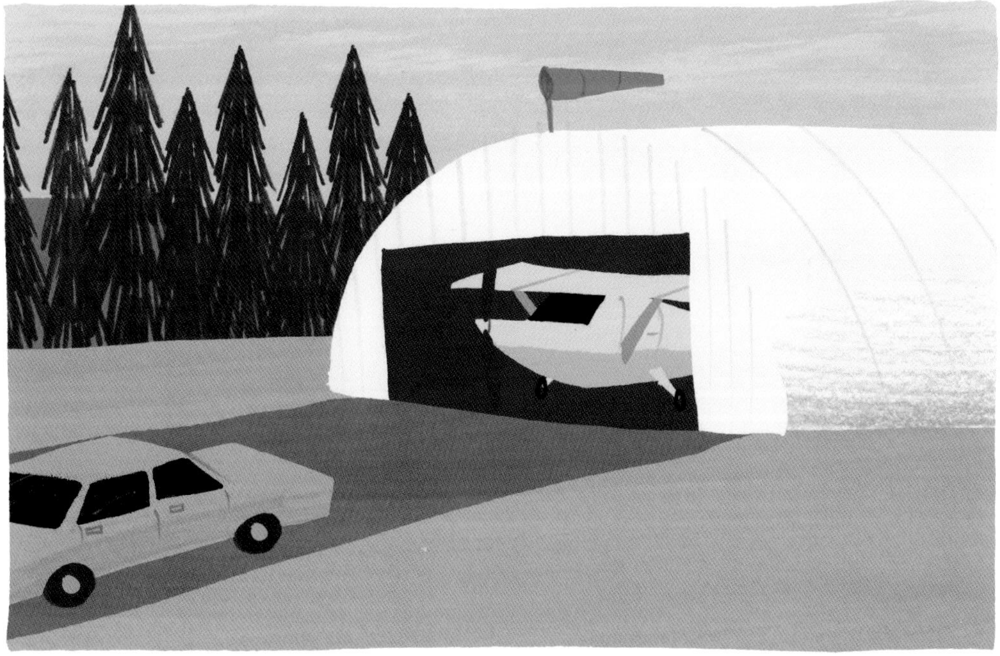

Meanwhile, on the ground, a federal agent was sent to retrieve the parachutes and the ransom money. The FBI was able to purchase two back parachutes and two front reserve chutes from SEATTLE SKY SPORTS, a skydiving school in nearby ISSAQUAH.

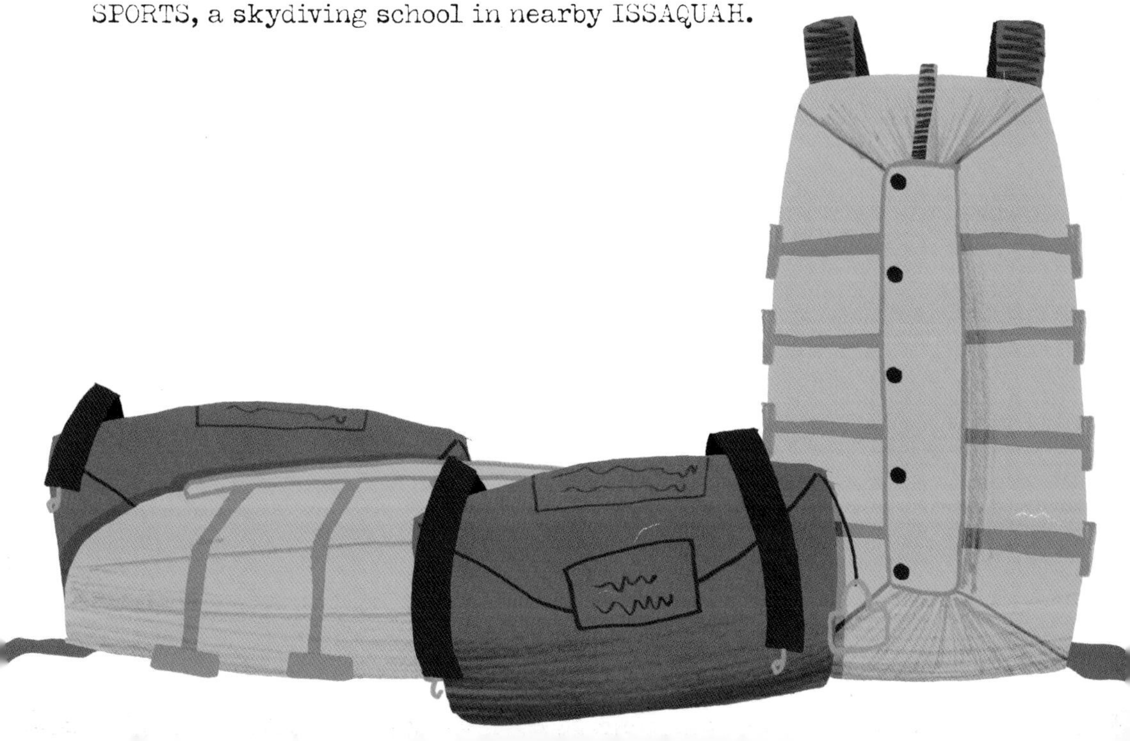

SEATTLE-FIRST NATIONAL BANK

The money was a little more complicated. It came from the SEATTLE FIRST NATIONAL BANK, which kept it earmarked for an emergency.

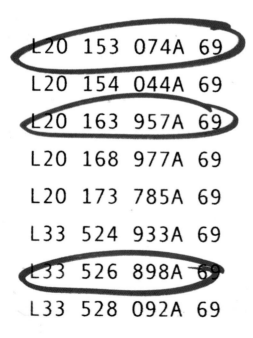

L20 153 074A 69

L20 154 044A 69

L20 163 957A 69

L20 168 977A 69

L20 173 785A 69

L33 524 933A 69

L33 526 898A 69

L33 528 092A 69

L33 529 797A 69

L33 530 471A 69

L33 532 853A 69

L54 899 276A 69

L54 904 730A 69

L54 907 155A 69

L54 929 823A 69

L54 984 623A 69

L54 986 729A 69

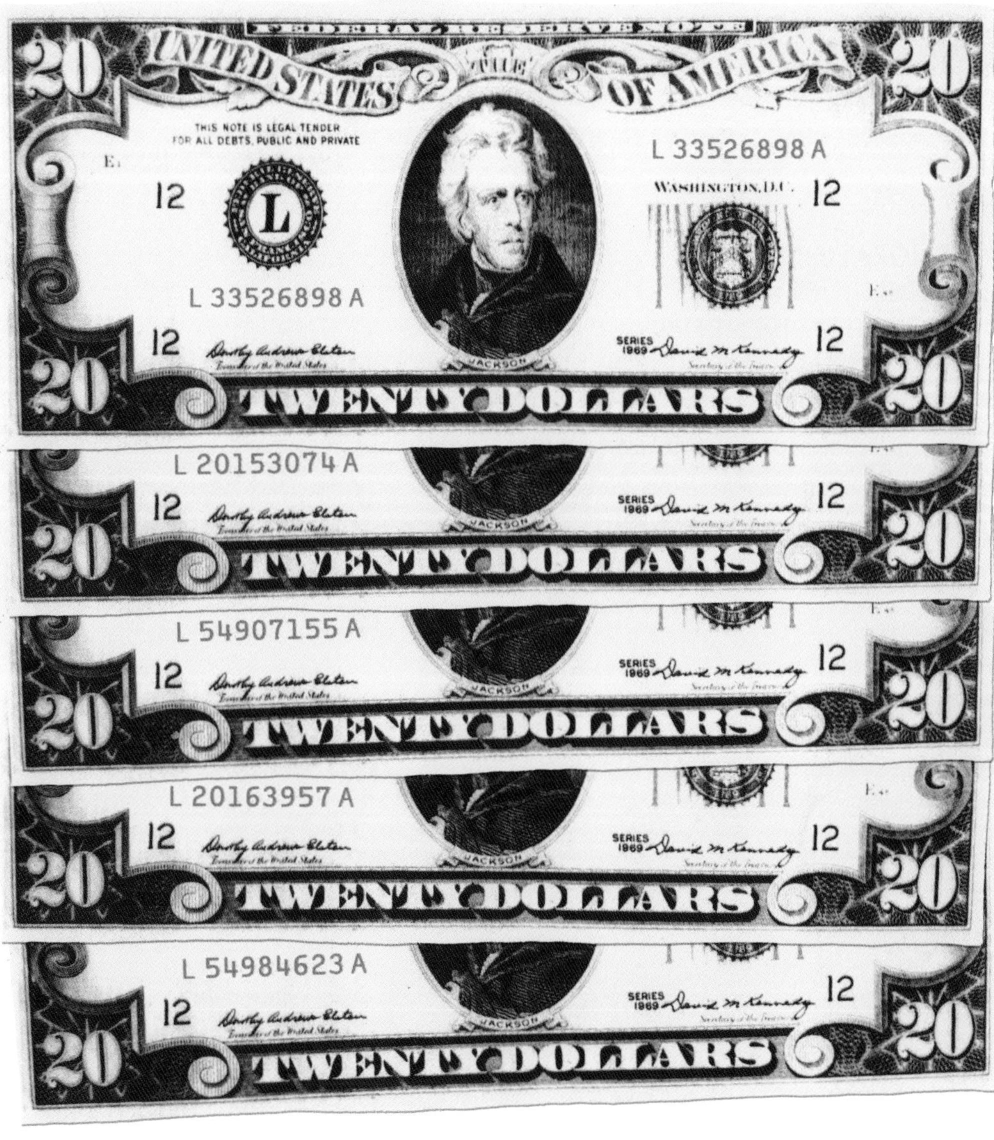
20
UNITED STATES OF AMERICA
THIS NOTE IS LEGAL TENDER FOR ALL DEBTS, PUBLIC AND PRIVATE
L 33526898 A
12
L
WASHINGTON, D.C.
L 33526898 A
SERIES 1969
JACKSON
TWENTY DOLLARS
L 20153074 A
L 54907155 A
L 20163957 A
L 54984623 A

In the case of a robbery, kidnapping, or ransom of any kind, the bank had $250,000 stored in random bundles, so that it would look like it was hastily gathered rather than prepared. They had also photographed and logged all the money's serial numbers. These serial numbers were then distributed to banks, casinos, and racetracks, and if anyone tried to deposit or spend the marked bills, the authorities would be able to track down and catch the perpetrator.

All the bills were from the 1969 series and were issued by the FEDERAL RESERVE BANK OF SAN FRANCISCO, as indicated by the letter *L*.

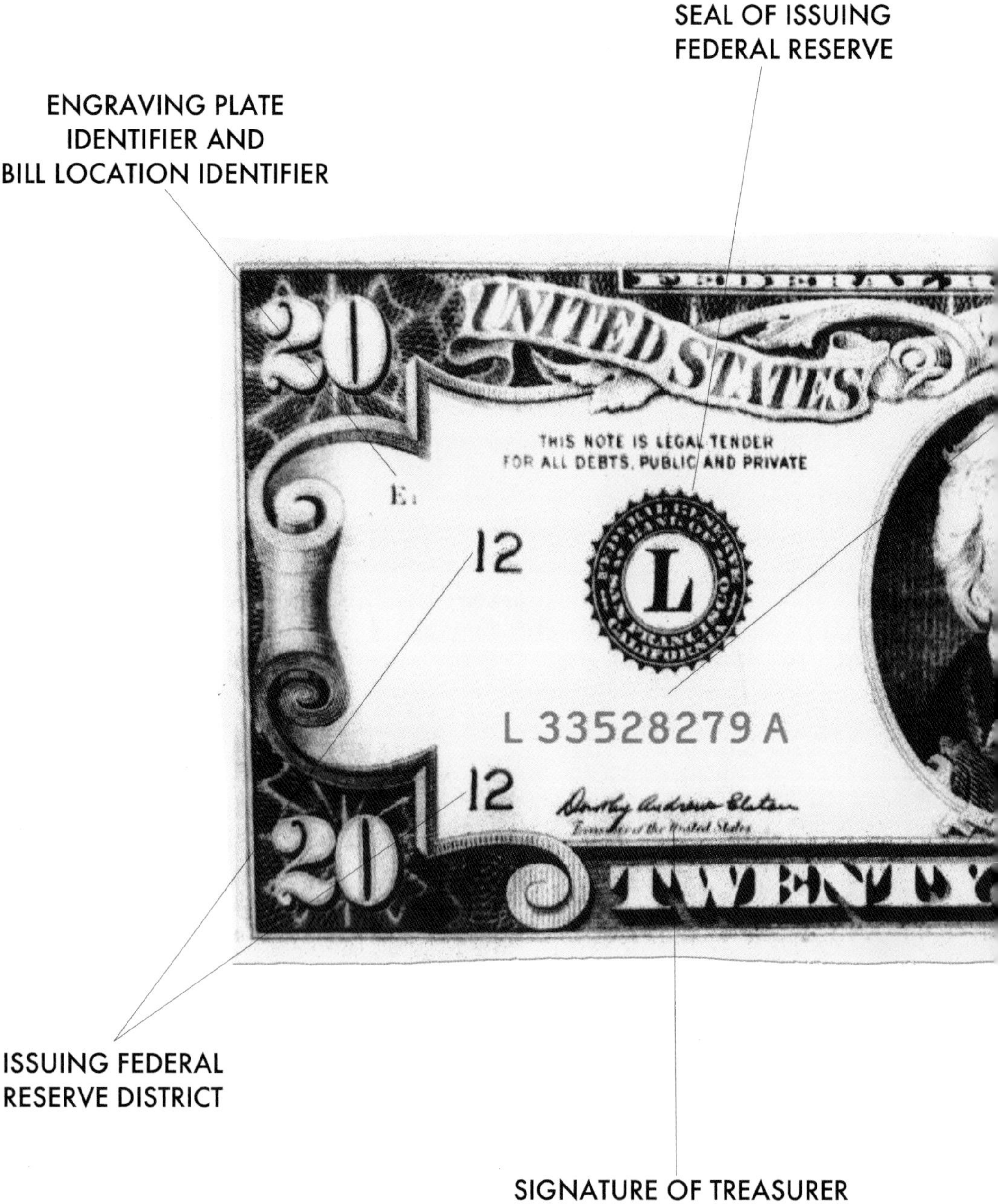
SEAL OF ISSUING
FEDERAL RESERVE
ENGRAVING PLATE
IDENTIFIER AND
BILL LOCATION IDENTIFIER
20
UNITED STATES
THIS NOTE IS LEGAL TENDER
FOR ALL DEBTS, PUBLIC AND PRIVATE
L
12
L 33528279 A
12
20
ISSUING FEDERAL
RESERVE DISTRICT
SIGNATURE OF TREASURER

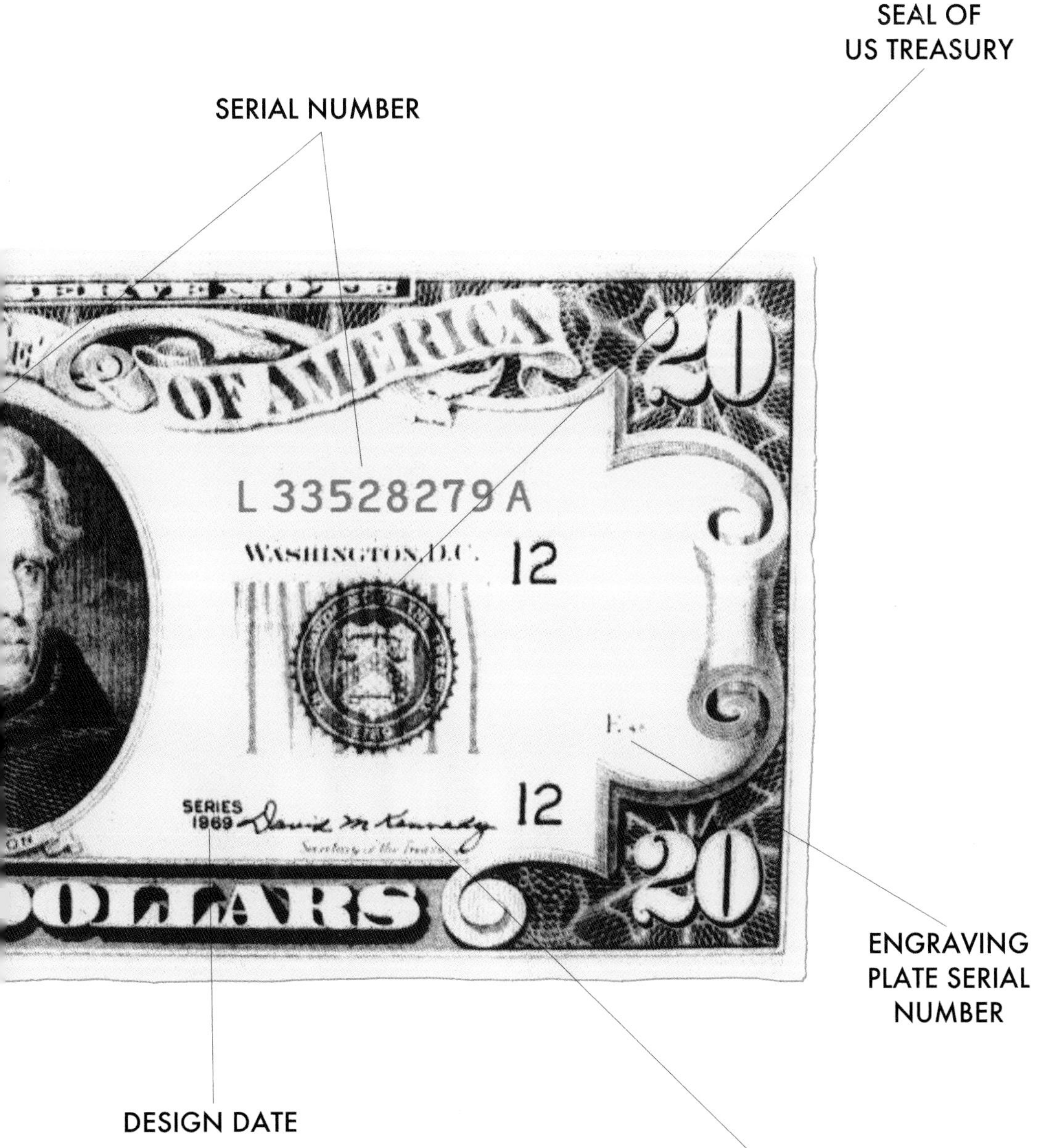
SEAL OF
US TREASURY
SERIAL NUMBER
OF AMERICA
20
L 33528279 A
WASHINGTON, D.C.
12
SERIES
1969
12
DOLLARS
20
ENGRAVING
PLATE SERIAL
NUMBER
DESIGN DATE
SIGNATURE OF TREASURY SECRETARY

5:39 p.m.

After almost two hours in a holding pattern over Washington, Flight 305 touched down on the tarmac in Seattle.

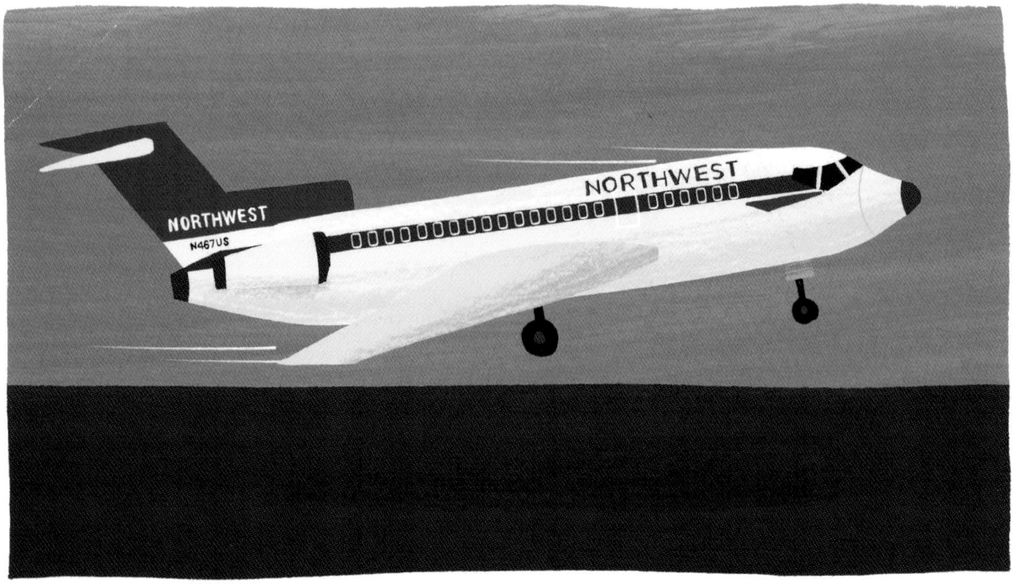
NORTHWEST
NORTHWEST
N467US

COOPER demanded that the airplane taxi to a remote section of the runway, where they would rendezvous with a stair car driven by a single airport employee.

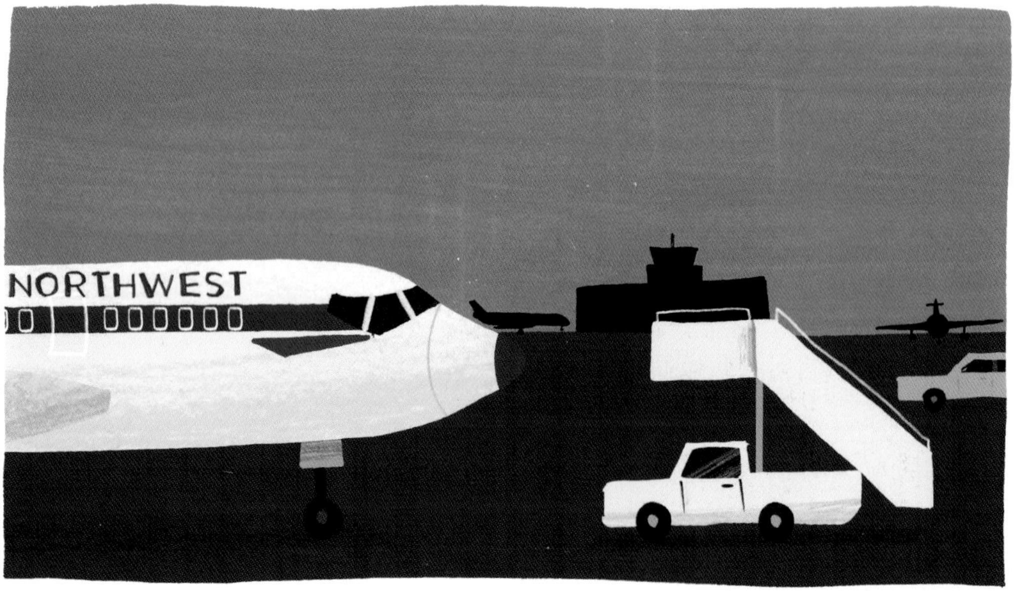
NORTHWEST

The captain told all the passengers to remain in their seats, while TINA MUCKLOW was sent to retrieve the money.

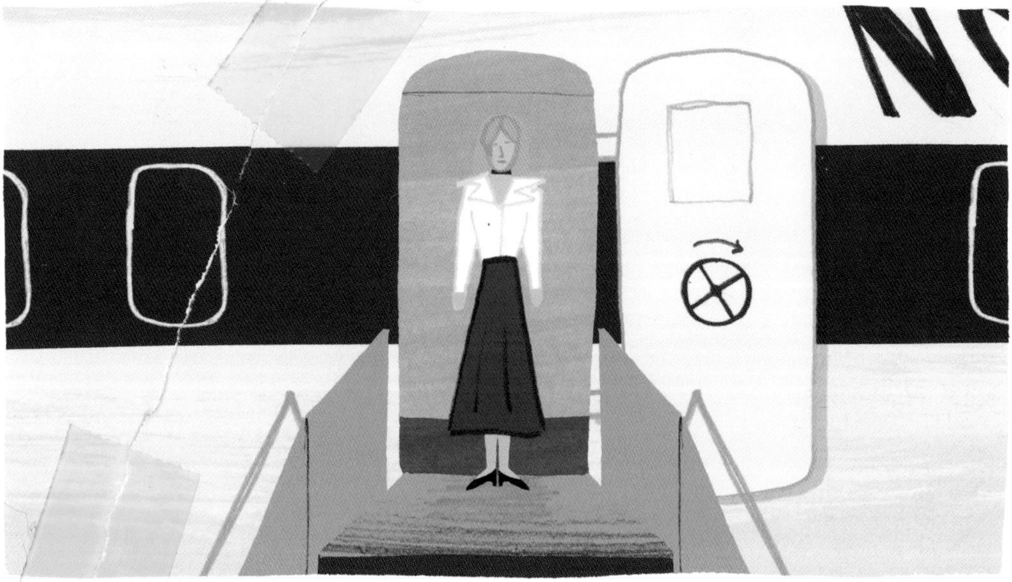

Waiting on the runway in a car that was visible from the aircraft was an FBI agent who handed the ransom to Ms. MUCKLOW.

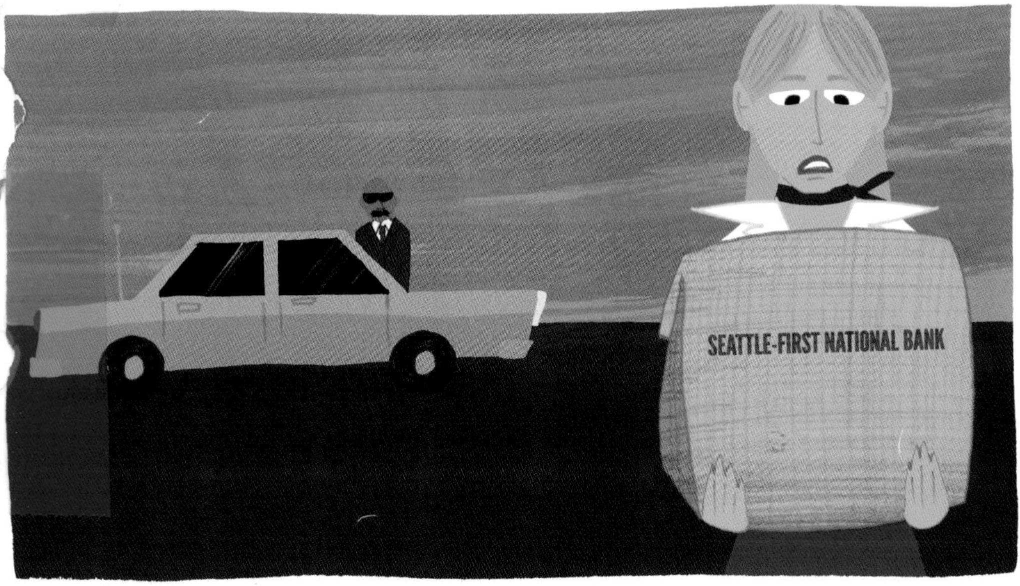
SEATTLE-FIRST NATIONAL BANK

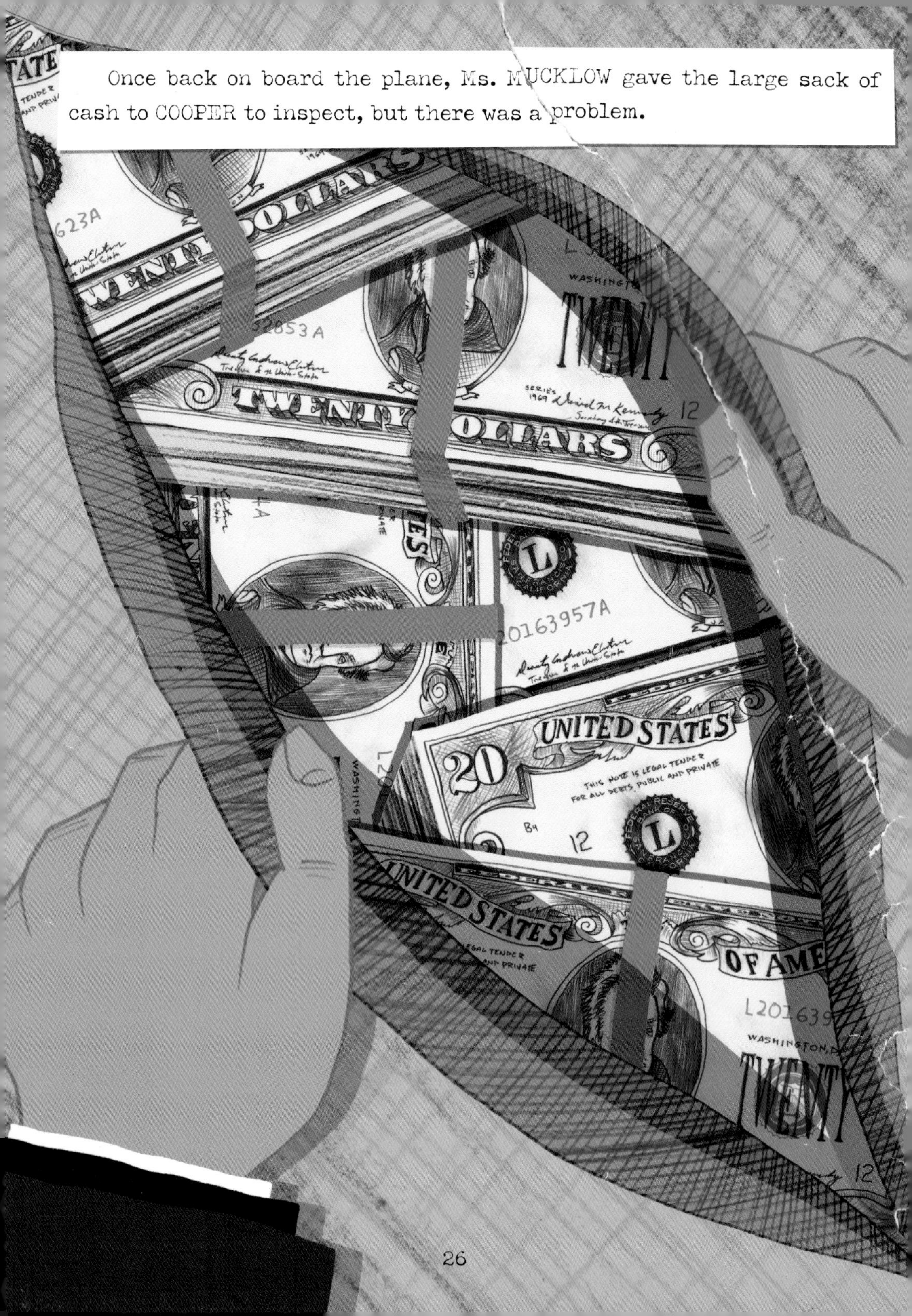
Once back on board the plane, Ms. MUCKLOW gave the large sack of cash to COOPER to inspect, but there was a problem.
TWENTY DOLLARS
TWENTY
L20163957A
UNITED STATES
20
THIS NOTE IS LEGAL TENDER FOR ALL DEBTS, PUBLIC AND PRIVATE
UNITED STATES
OF AME

He hadn't specified the denomination that he wanted the money to come in. So instead of getting the $200,000 in 2,000 one-hundred-dollar bills, he got it in 10,000 twenty-dollar bills. The money also arrived in a large canvas bank bag instead of the requested knapsack.

If a dollar bill weighs one gram, then 10,000 dollar bills weigh just a hair over twenty-two pounds. That may not sound like too much at first, but imagine trying to jump out of an airplane with two bowling balls strapped to your chest.

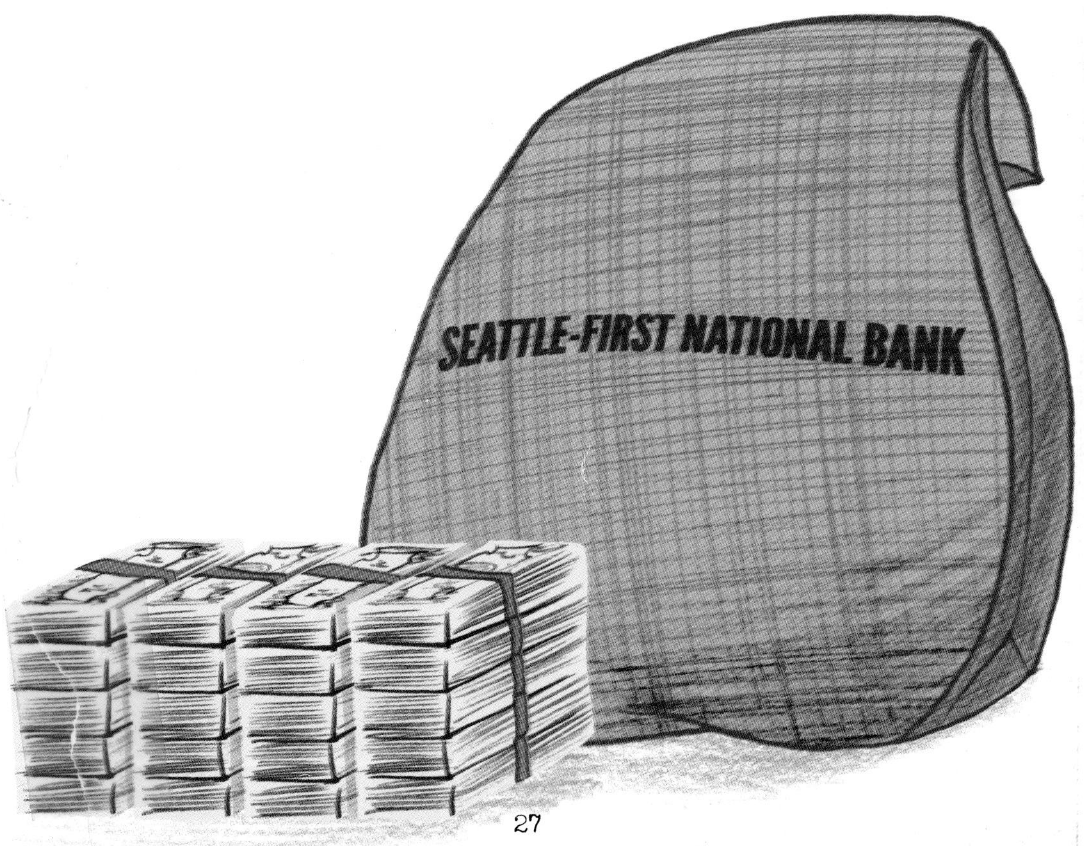
SEATTLE-FIRST NATIONAL BANK

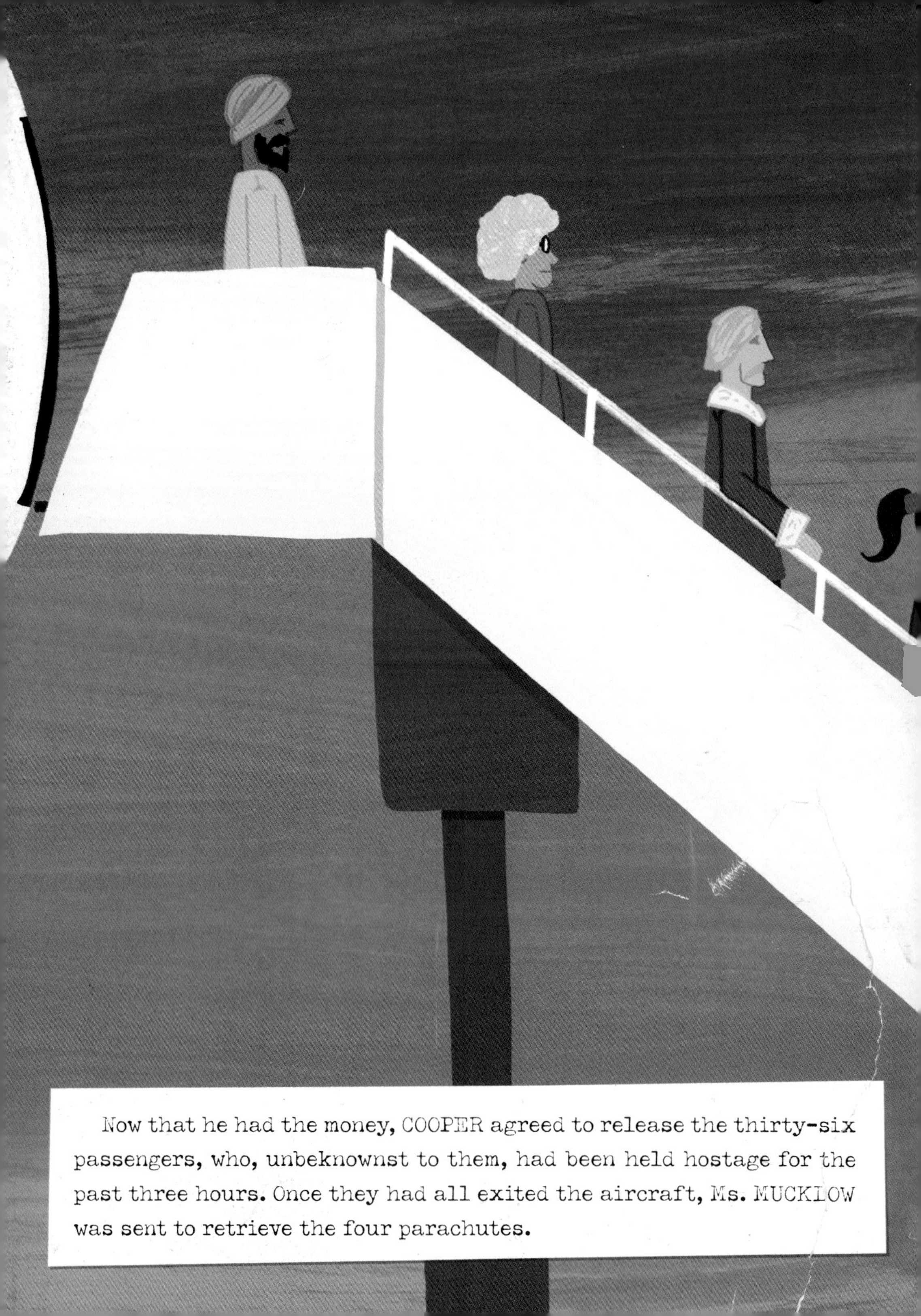

Now that he had the money, COOPER agreed to release the thirty-six passengers, who, unbeknownst to them, had been held hostage for the past three hours. Once they had all exited the aircraft, Ms. MUCKLOW was sent to retrieve the four parachutes.

After the parachutes were on board, COOPER had all the window shades pulled down so that a sniper wouldn't be able to shoot at him.

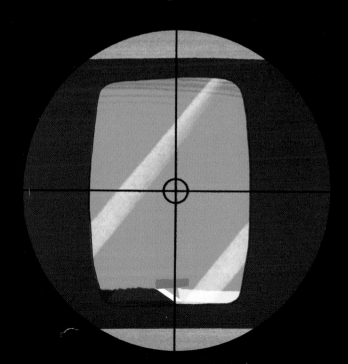

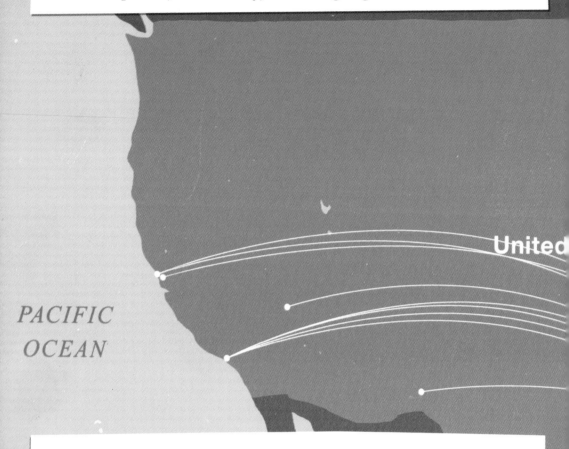

Nervously, Ms. MUCKLOW asked where they were going next, to which COOPER responded, "Don't worry, we're not going to Havana."

PACIFIC
OCEAN

United

During the late 1960s and early 1970s, airplane hijacking—or "sky-jacking"—was something of an epidemic in the United States. In fact, due to the hostile relationship between the US and CUBA at the time, from 1968 through 1971, there were over eighty recorded instances where individuals hijacked planes and directed them to fly to Cuba.

Some of these hijackers were simply terrorists or criminals, but others were politically motivated. During the Cold War—and up until very recently—there was a travel embargo in place, meaning that civilians couldn't legally fly between the two countries. That, however, did not stop some communist sympathizers from going to extreme lengths in order to migrate to Cuba.

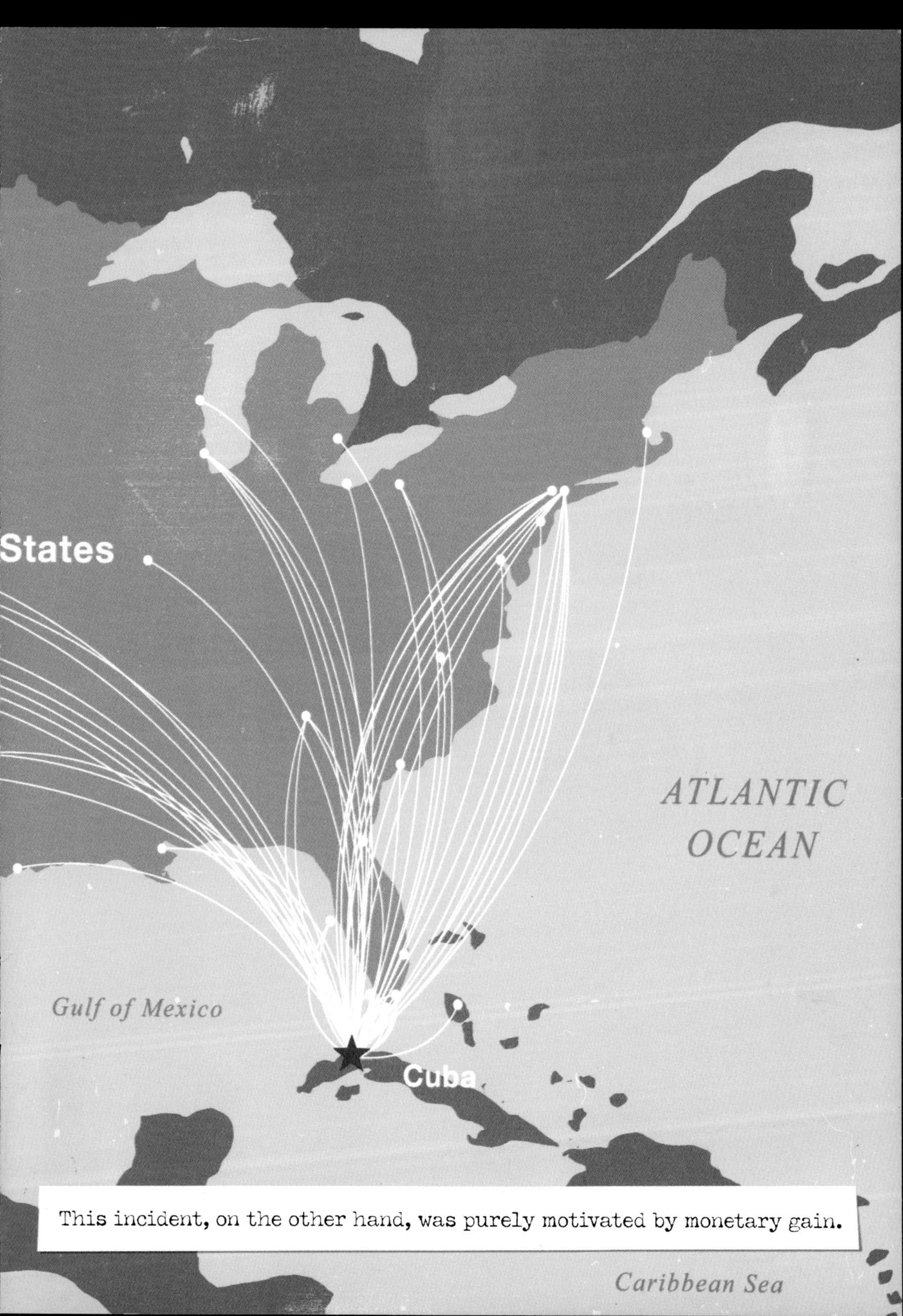
States
ATLANTIC
OCEAN
Gulf of Mexico
Cuba
Caribbean Sea

This incident, on the other hand, was purely motivated by monetary gain.

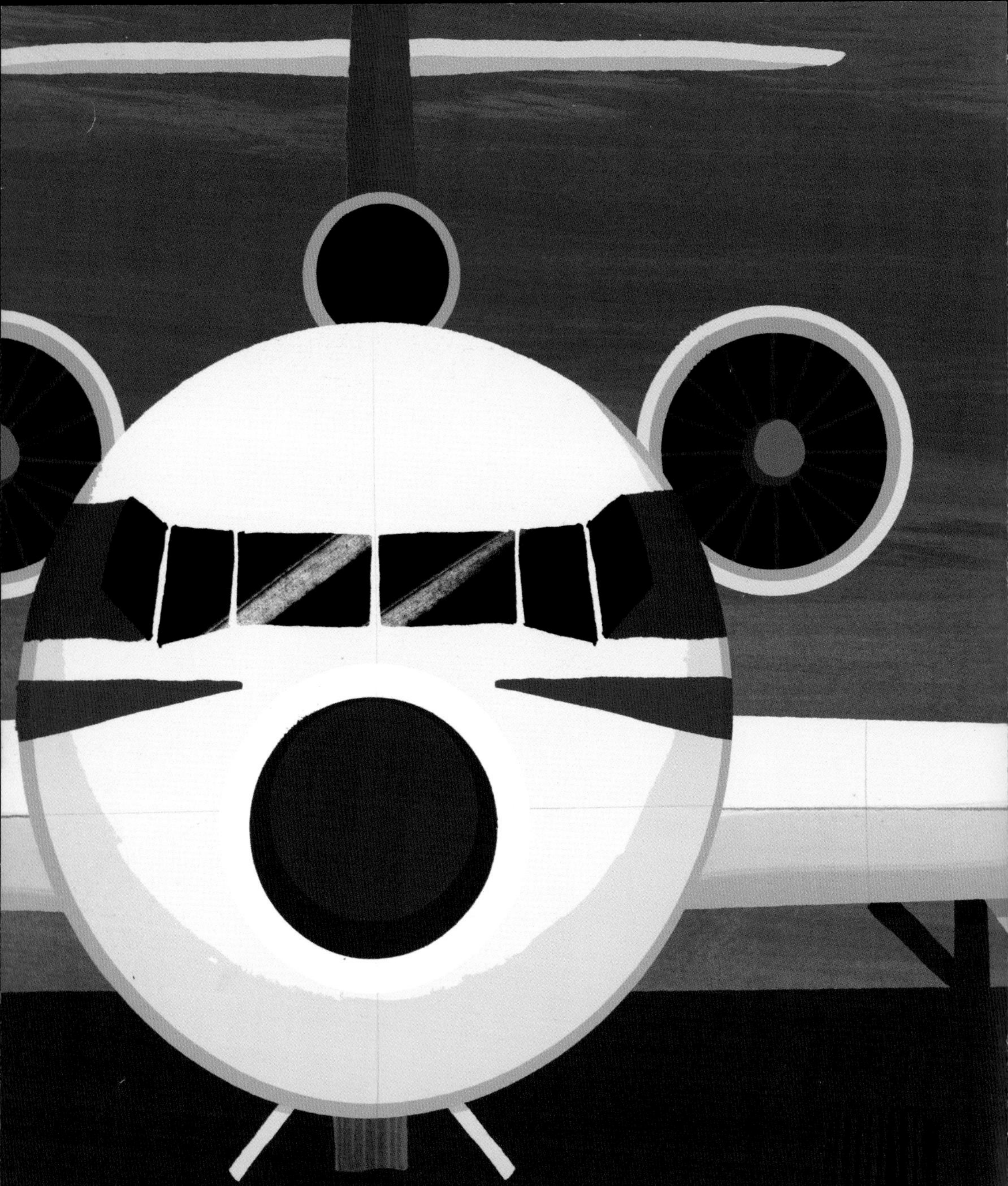

PART THREE:
THE ESCAPE

While the plane was refueling, COOPER relayed to the pilot his next set of demands. He wanted the plane to set a course for MEXICO CITY, but he wanted the plane to fly with the landing gear deployed, at the lowest possible speed, at a maximum of 10,000 feet. (Typically, commercial planes fly at around 35,000 feet.) COOPER also wanted the plane to take off with the aft (rear) staircase lowered.

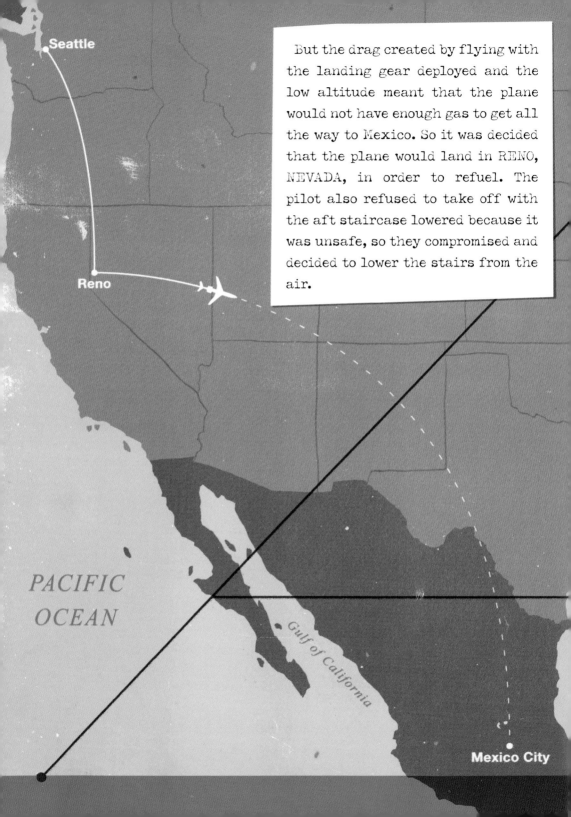

Seattle

Reno

But the drag created by flying with the landing gear deployed and the low altitude meant that the plane would not have enough gas to get all the way to Mexico. So it was decided that the plane would land in RENO, NEVADA, in order to refuel. The pilot also refused to take off with the aft staircase lowered because it was unsafe, so they compromised and decided to lower the stairs from the air.

PACIFIC OCEAN

Gulf of California

Mexico City

40,000 FT –

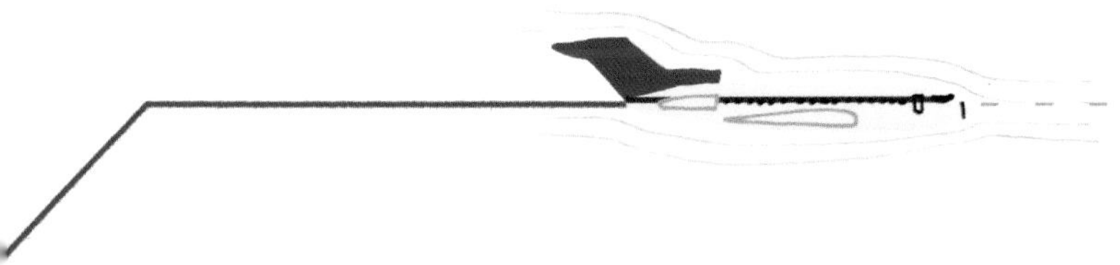

Airplanes are designed with an aerodynamic shape so that they can smoothly travel through the air. However, if something clunky—like landing gear—is added to the equation, it creates friction known as drag. And more drag means more power is needed, and more power means more fuel.

20,000 FT –

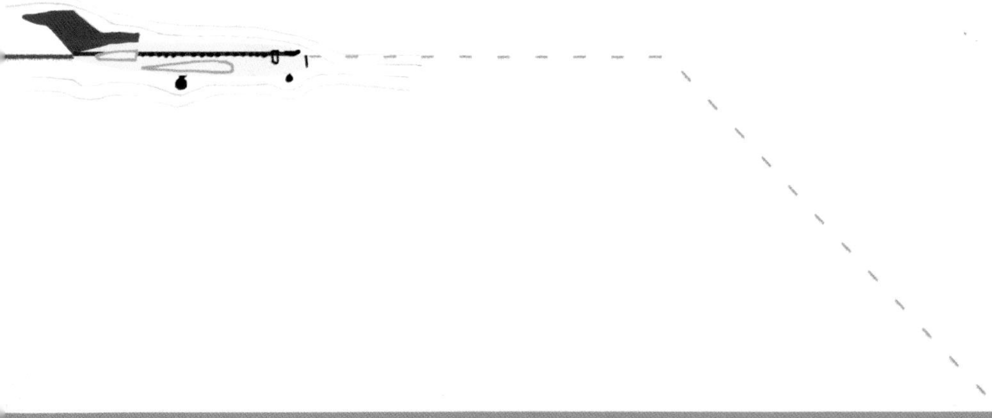

Boeing 727-100
Aft Stairs

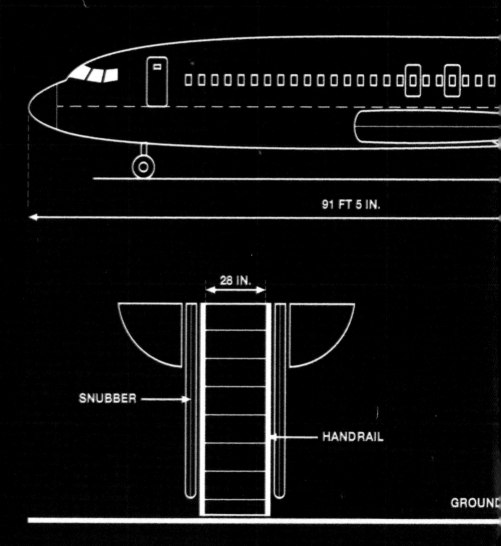

91 FT 5 IN.

28 IN.

SNUBBER

HANDRAIL

GROUND

REAR VIEW

The whole reason that COOPER hijacked Northwest Orient Airlines Flight 305 in the first place was that it was a Boeing 727, which at the time was the only commercial plane that had a rear staircase. Since the 727 was relatively small in terms of jetliners, it was usually used for shorter flights. The purpose of the stairs was to improve turn-around times: while passengers were deplaning from the front, the aircraft could be cleaned and restocked from the rear.

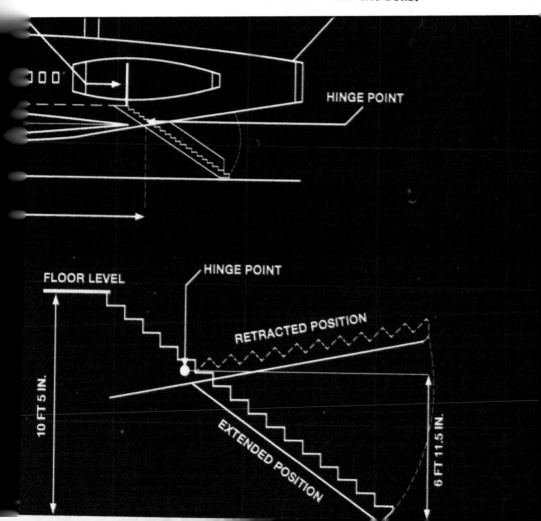

HINGE POINT

FLOOR LEVEL

HINGE POINT

RETRACTED POSITION

EXTENDED POSITION

10 FT 5 IN.

6 FT 11.5 IN.

7:36 p.m.

Taking off into a chilly 40-degree rainstorm, Flight 305 departed from Seattle for Reno with five people on board.

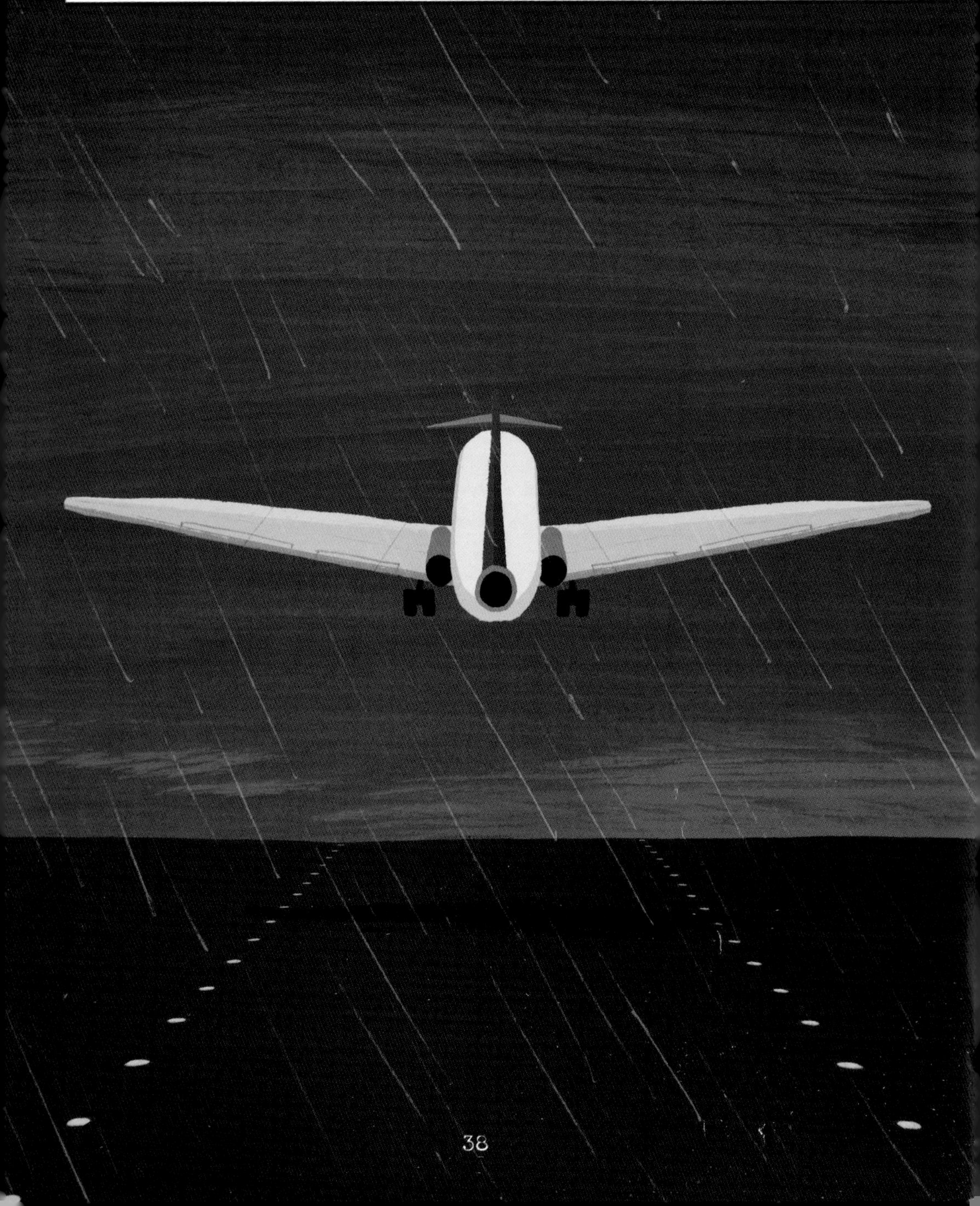

They were the pilot, Captain WILLIAM SCOTT, first officer WILLIAM RATACZAK, flight engineer HAROLD E. ANDERSON, flight attendant TINA MUCKLOW, and the hijacker, DAN COOPER.

CAPT. W. SCOTT

W. RATACZAK

H. ANDERSON

T. MUCKLOW

D. COOPER

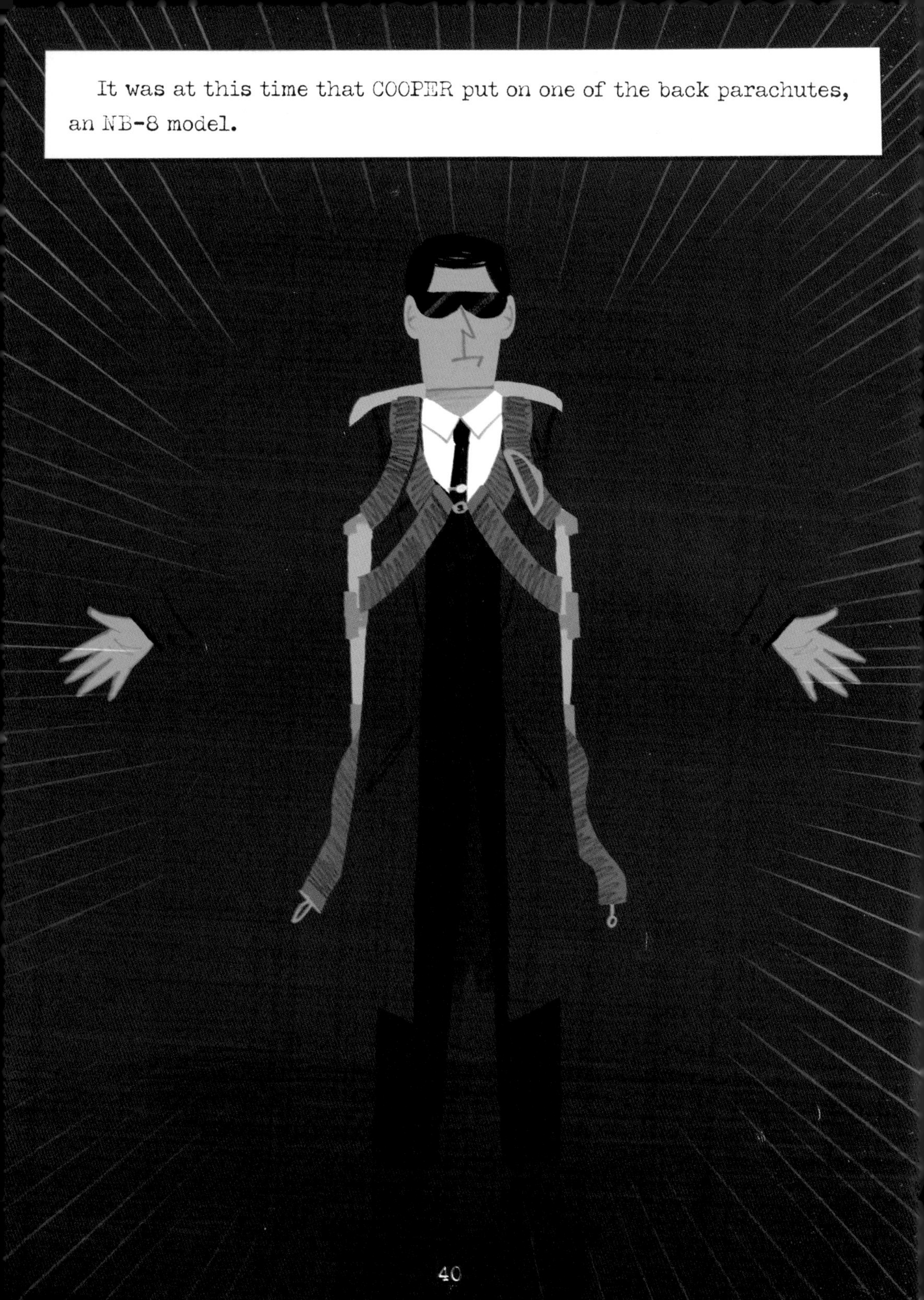
It was at this time that COOPER put on one of the back parachutes, an NB-8 model.

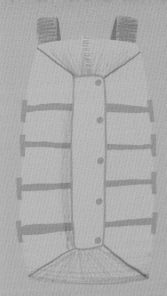

He also opened up one of the front parachutes, which was meant to be an emergency backup chute, and cut the nylon cords with a pocket-knife. Because the money had been delivered in a bank bag, there was no handle, so COOPER had to fashion one.

COOPER'S choice of para-chutes remains a point of contention to this day. The parachute he chose to wear on his back, the NB-8, was a military-style parachute designed for emergency ejections. This was not meant for para-chuting or skydiving, and it did not have the ability to be steered. The Pioneer sport parachute—which he had cut open—would have been better suited for sky-diving.

All this goes to suggest that even though COOPER was familiar with the con-cept of parachuting, he was not an experienced para-trooper.

SE[ ]TLE-FIRST NATIONAL BA[ ]K

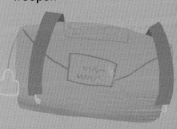

Meanwhile, the air force had dispatched two F-106 fighter jets and a Lockheed HC-130 to follow Flight 305. But due to the low speeds and poor weather, they were unable to maintain a visual on the hijacked 727.

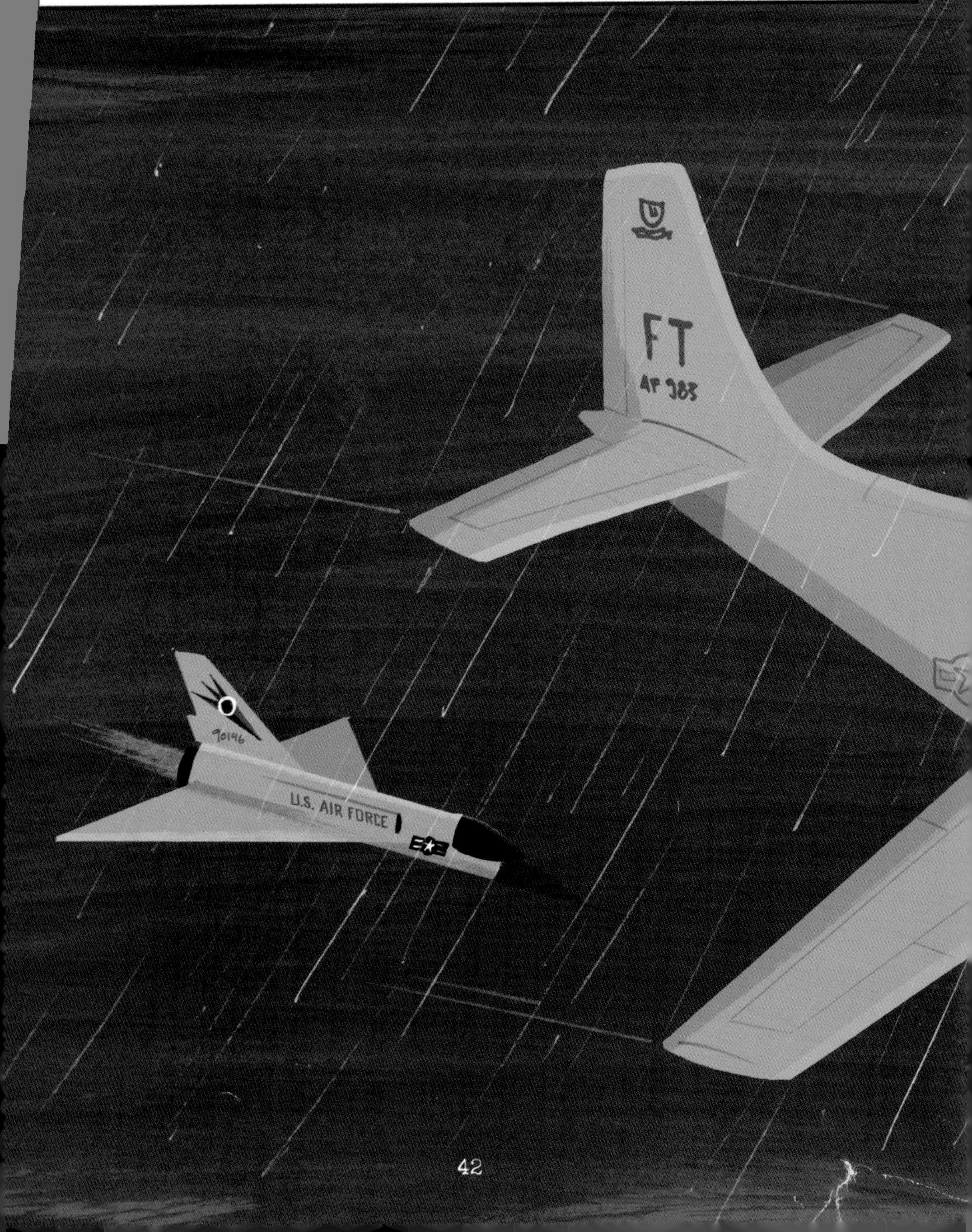
FT
AF 983
96146
U.S. AIR FORCE

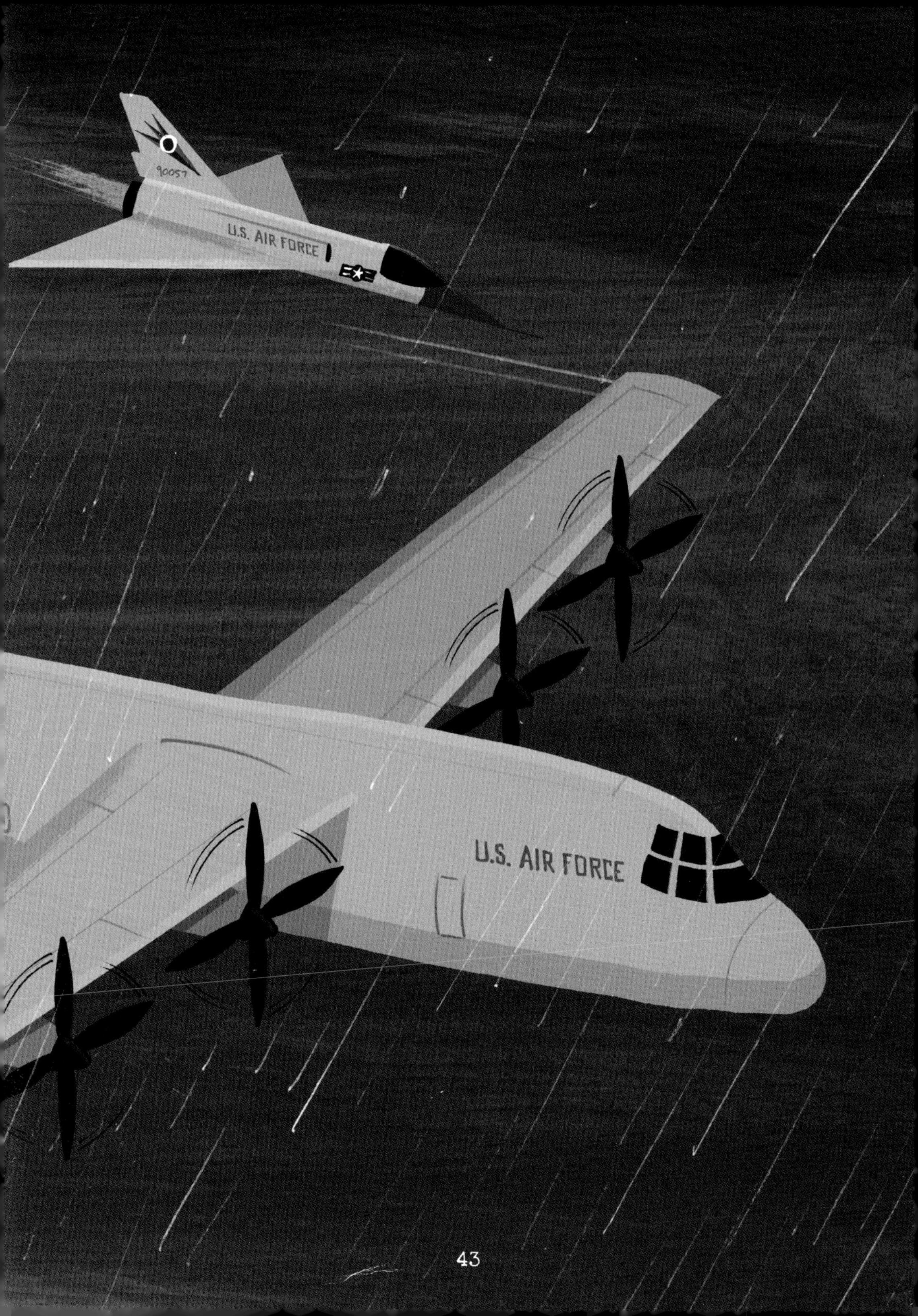
90057
U.S. AIR FORCE
U.S. AIR FORCE

7:41 p.m.

COOPER'S original plan was to have TINA MUCKLOW lower the rear staircase, but after she voiced her fear of falling out of the airplane, he instructed that she go to the cockpit, and that no one set foot beyond the first-class area.

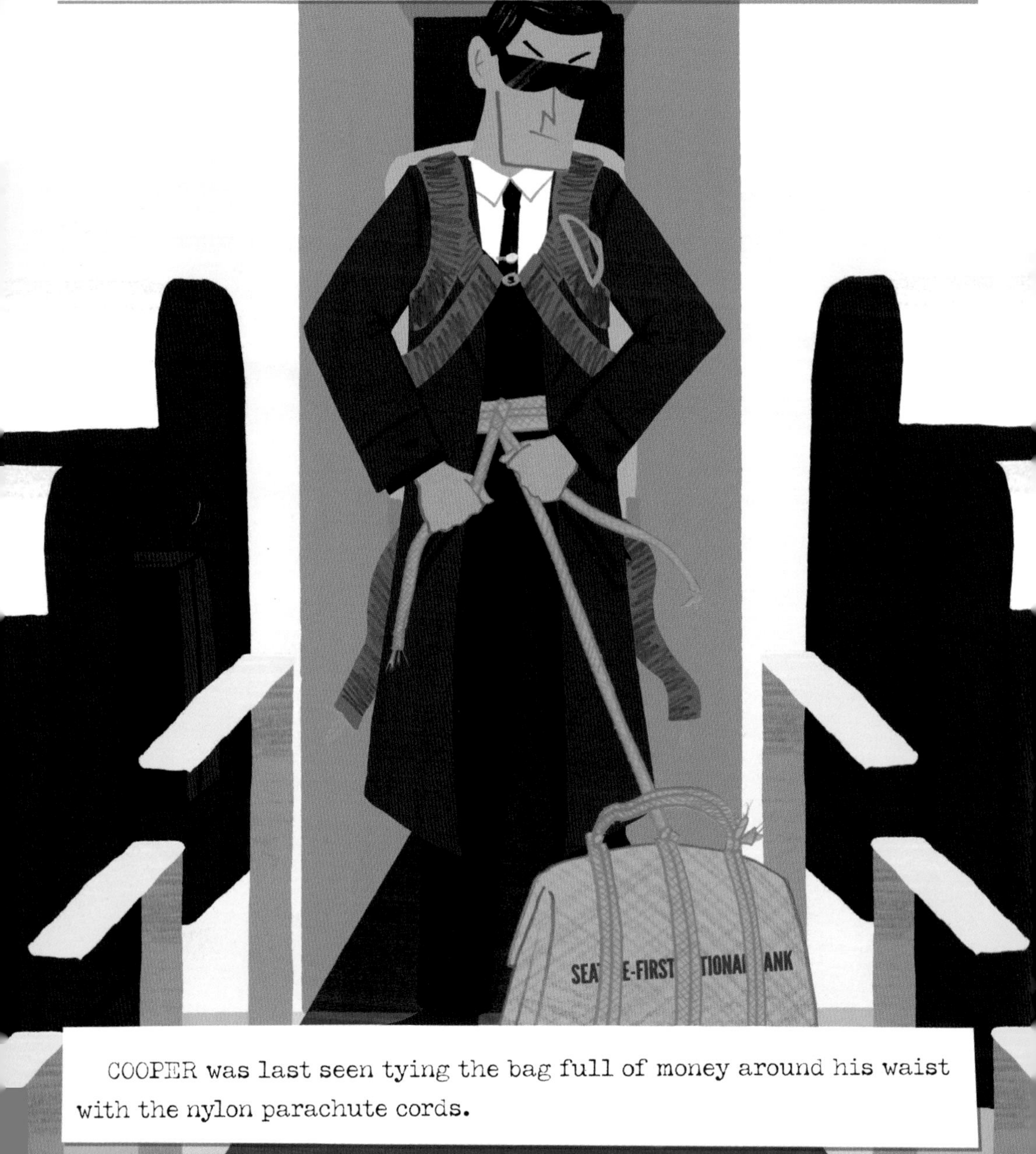

COOPER was last seen tying the bag full of money around his waist with the nylon parachute cords.

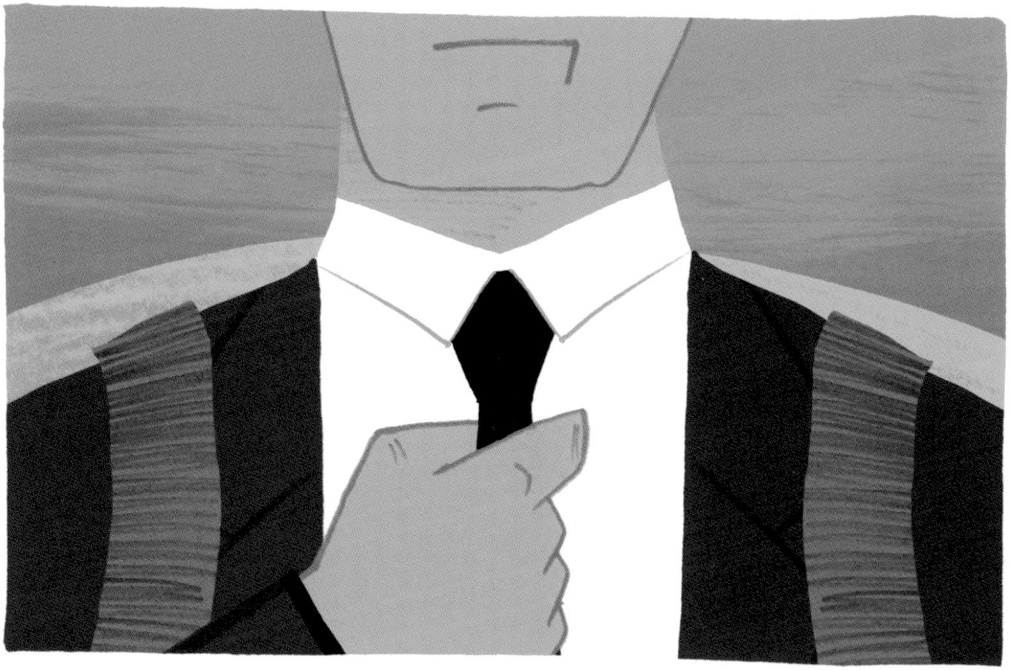

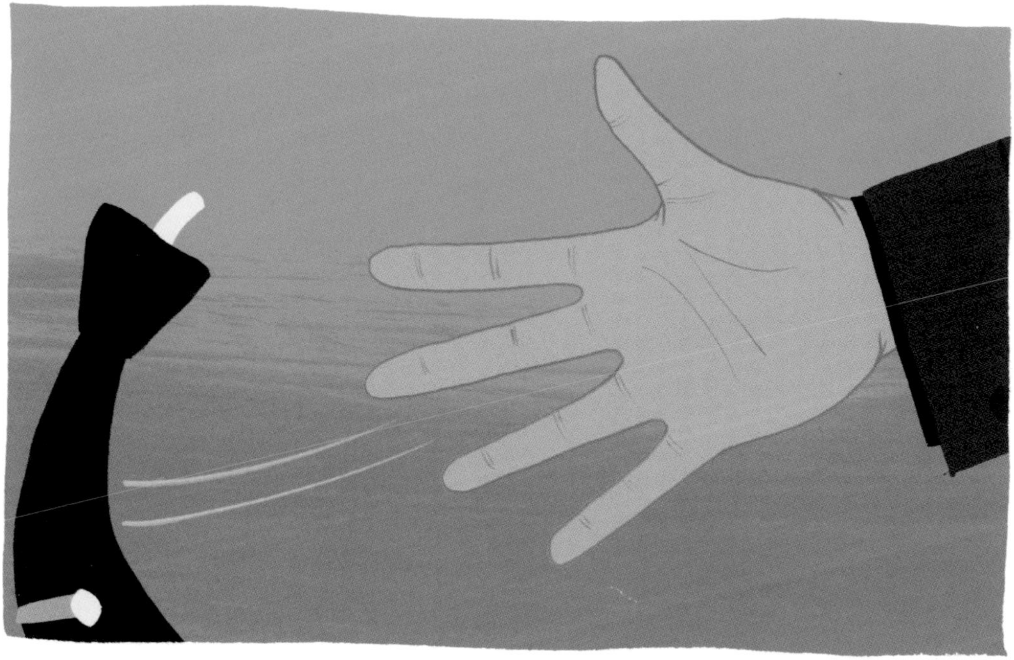

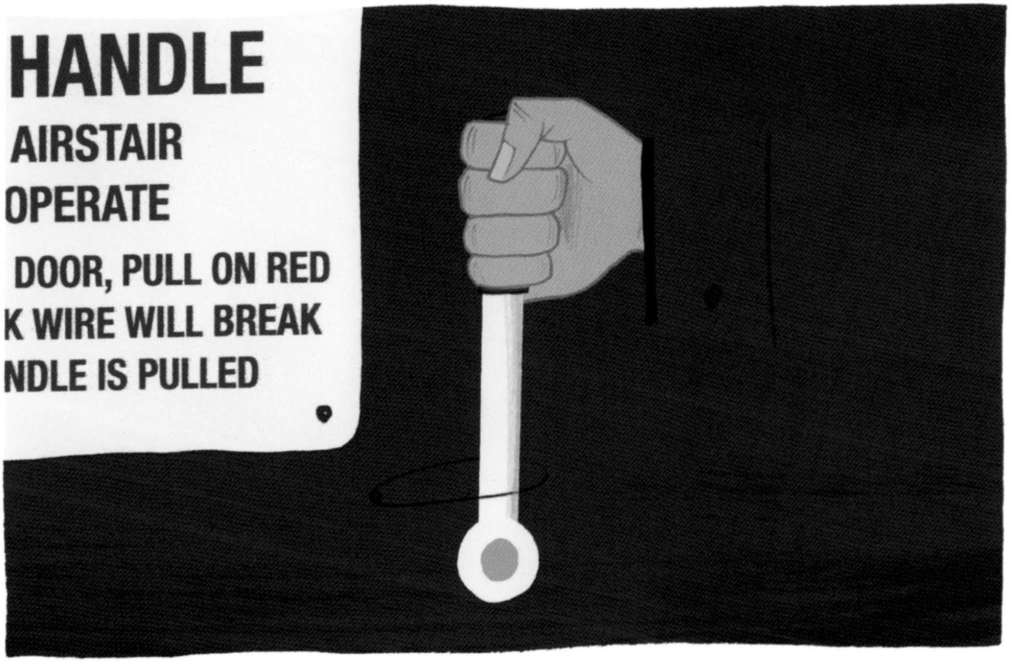
HANDLE
AIRSTAIR
OPERATE
DOOR, PULL ON RED
K WIRE WILL BREAK
NDLE IS PULLED

7:43 p.m.

A warning light flashed in the cockpit, indicating that the aft stairs had been lowered.

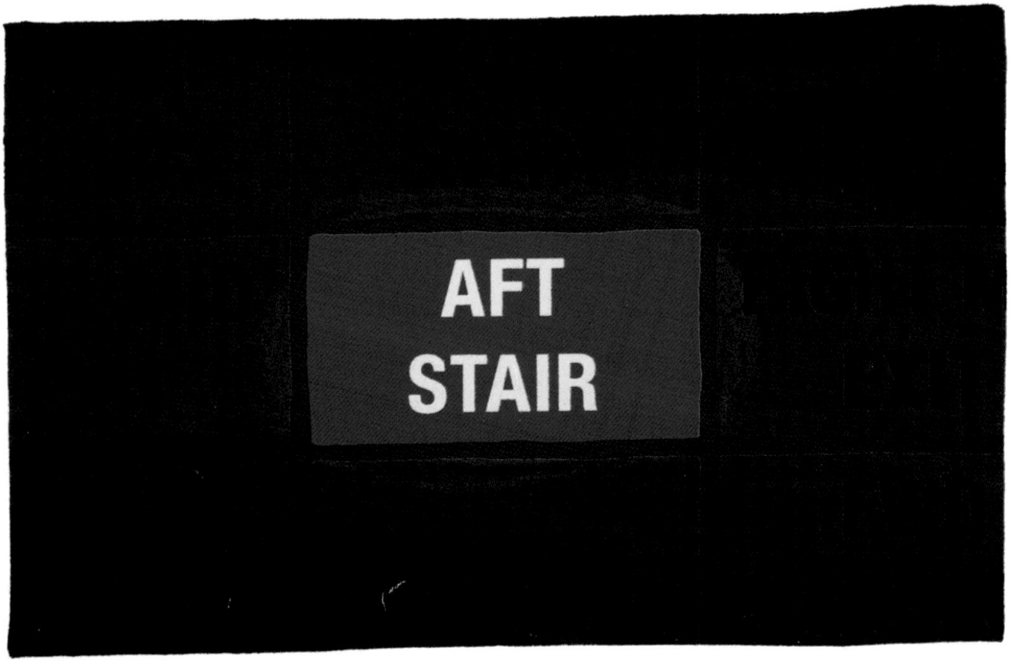
AFT
STAIR

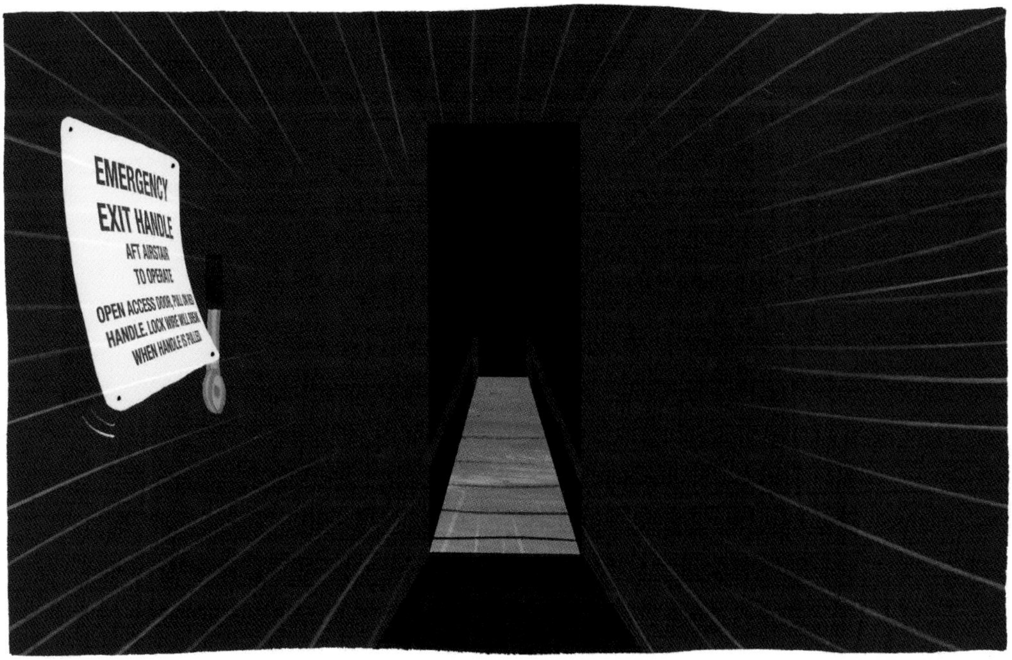
EMERGENCY
EXIT HANDLE
AFT AIRSTAIR
TO OPERATE
OPEN ACCESS DOOR,
HANDLE. LOCK WIRE WILL
WHEN HANDLE IS

Immediately, a plastic instructional placard was sucked out of the plane, confirming Ms. MUCKLOW'S worst fears.

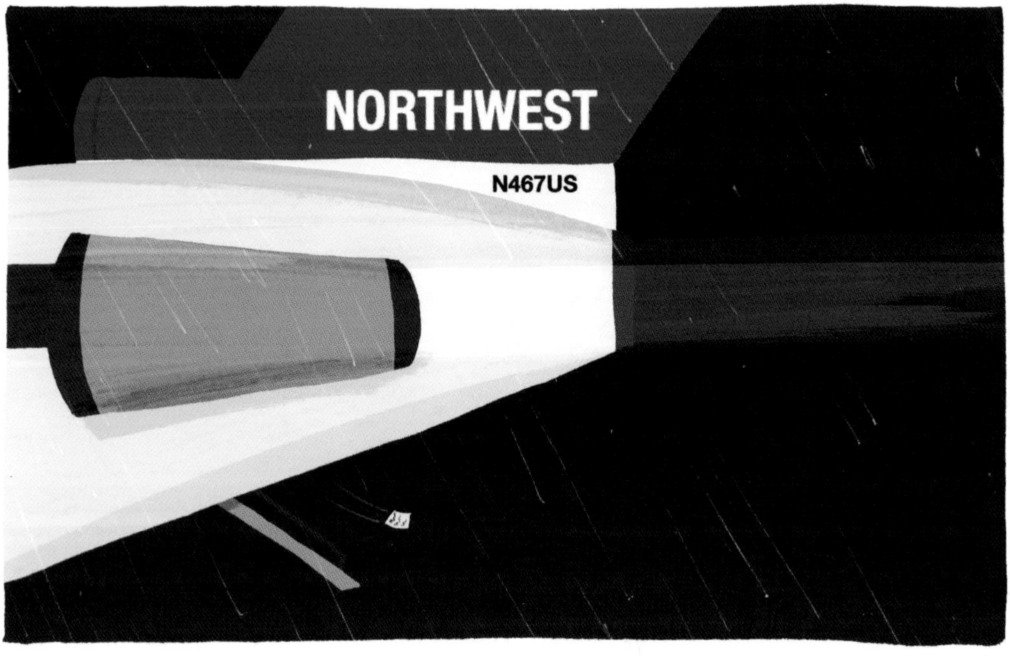
NORTHWEST
N467US

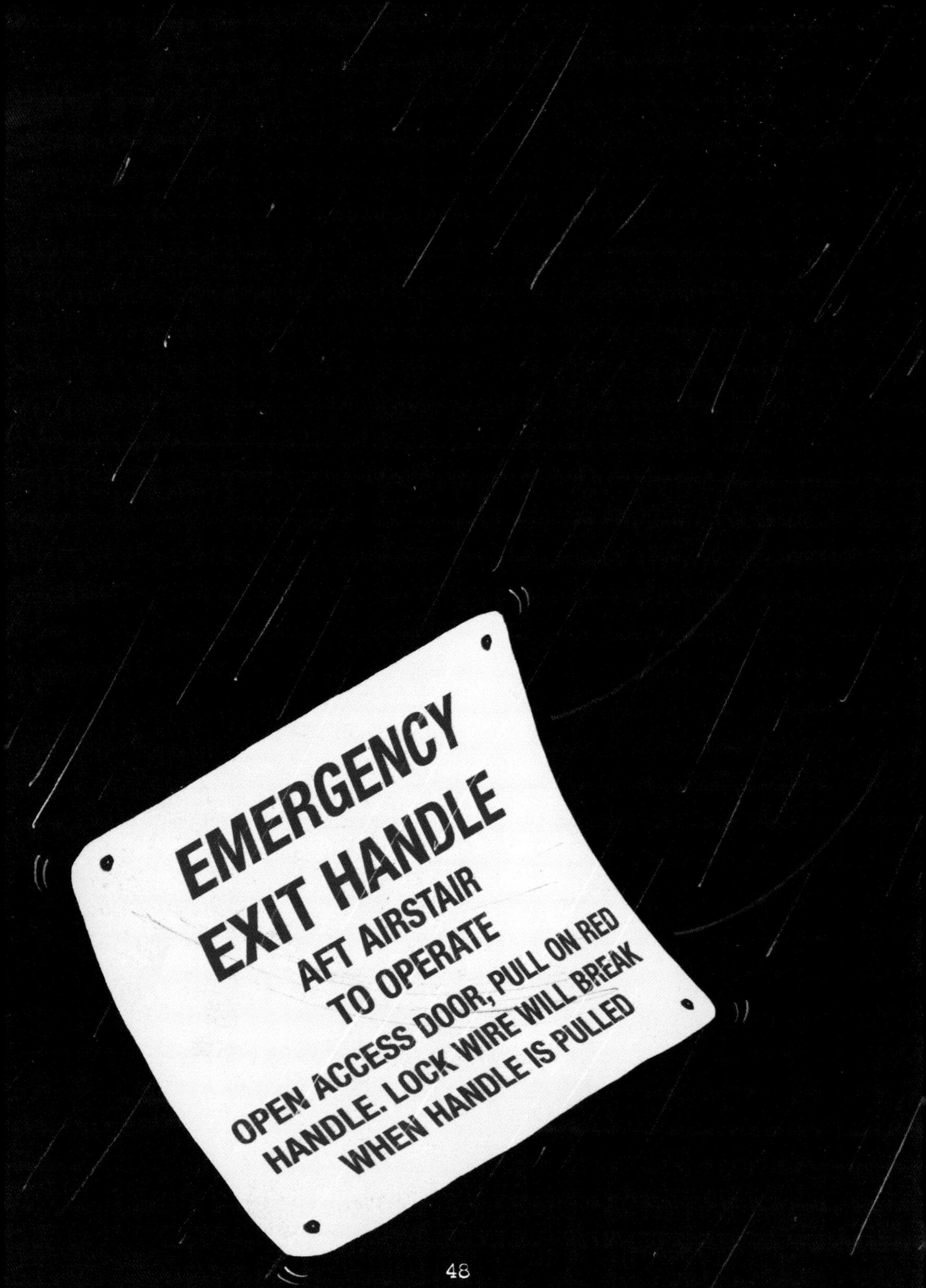
EMERGENCY
EXIT HANDLE
AFT AIRSTAIR
TO OPERATE
OPEN ACCESS DOOR, PULL ON RED
HANDLE. LOCK WIRE WILL BREAK
WHEN HANDLE IS PULLED

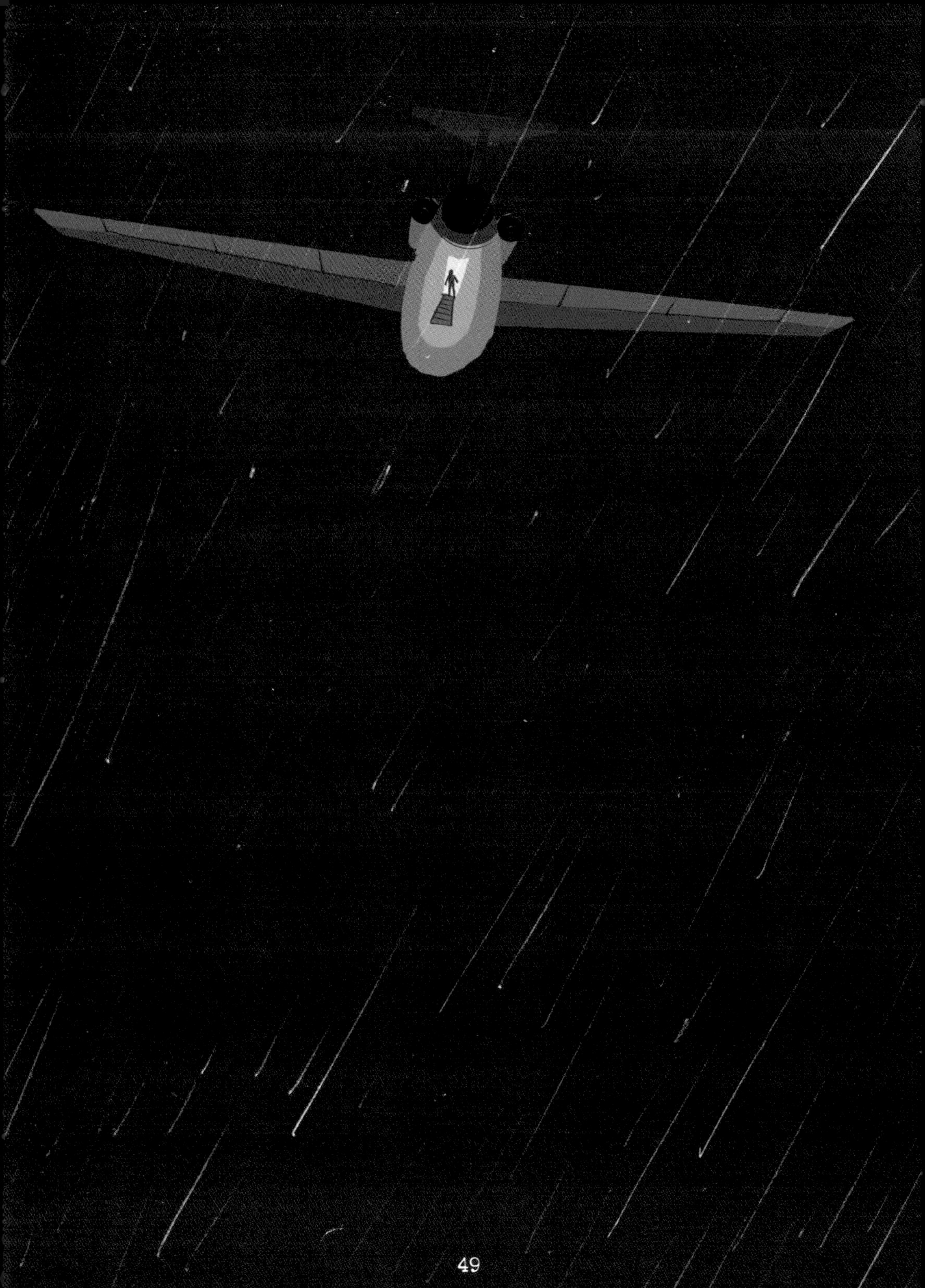

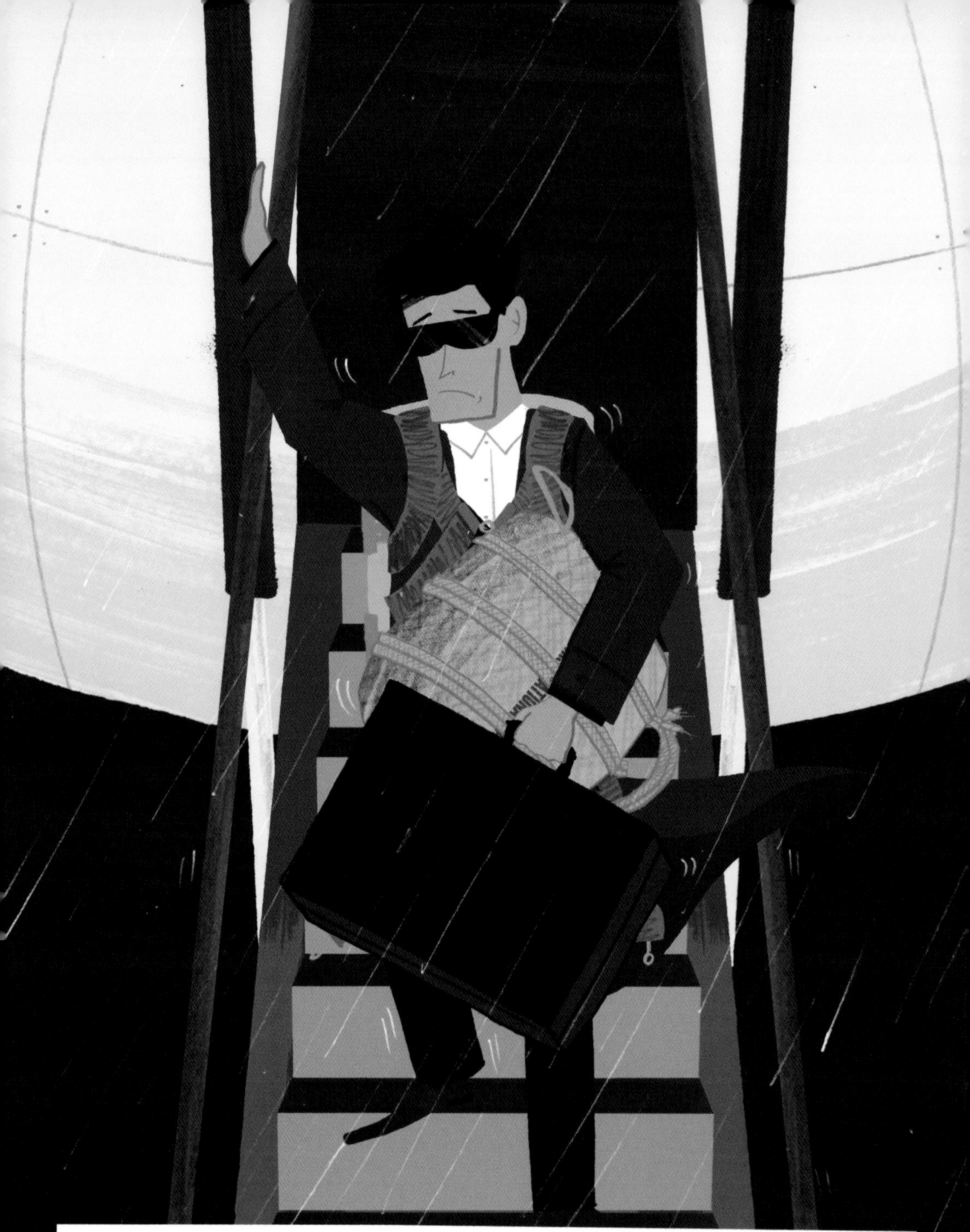

Clutching the bag full of money, COOPER slowly descended the stairs as the wind and rain whipped around him.

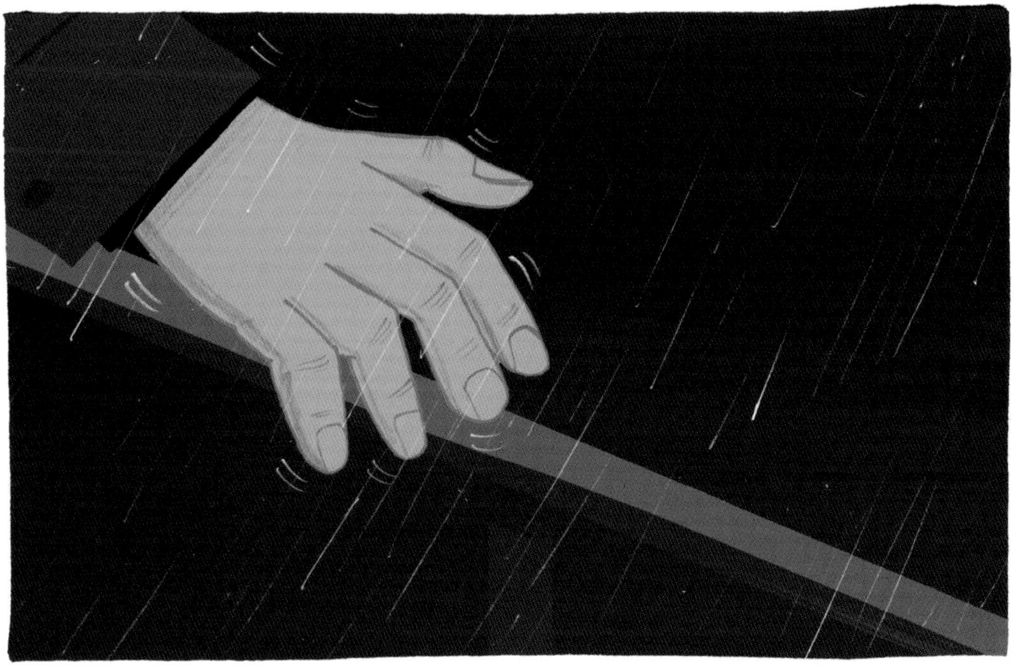

8:03 p.m.

The external temperature was recorded as being -7 degrees Celsius (19.4 degrees Fahrenheit).

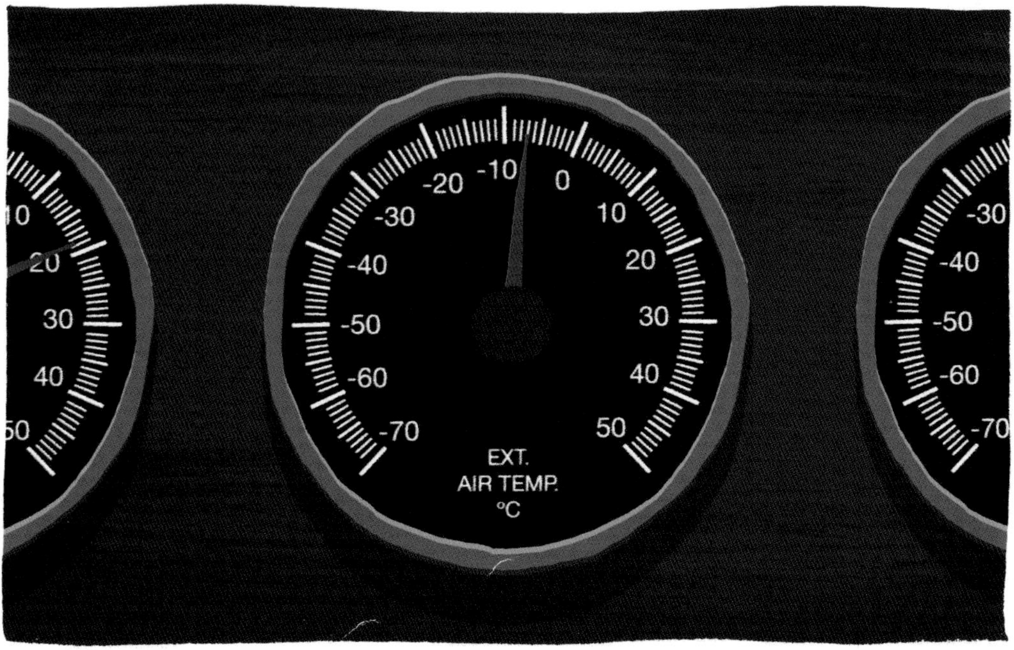

-70
-60
-50
-40
-30
-20
-10
0
10
20
30
40
50
EXT.
AIR TEMP.
°C

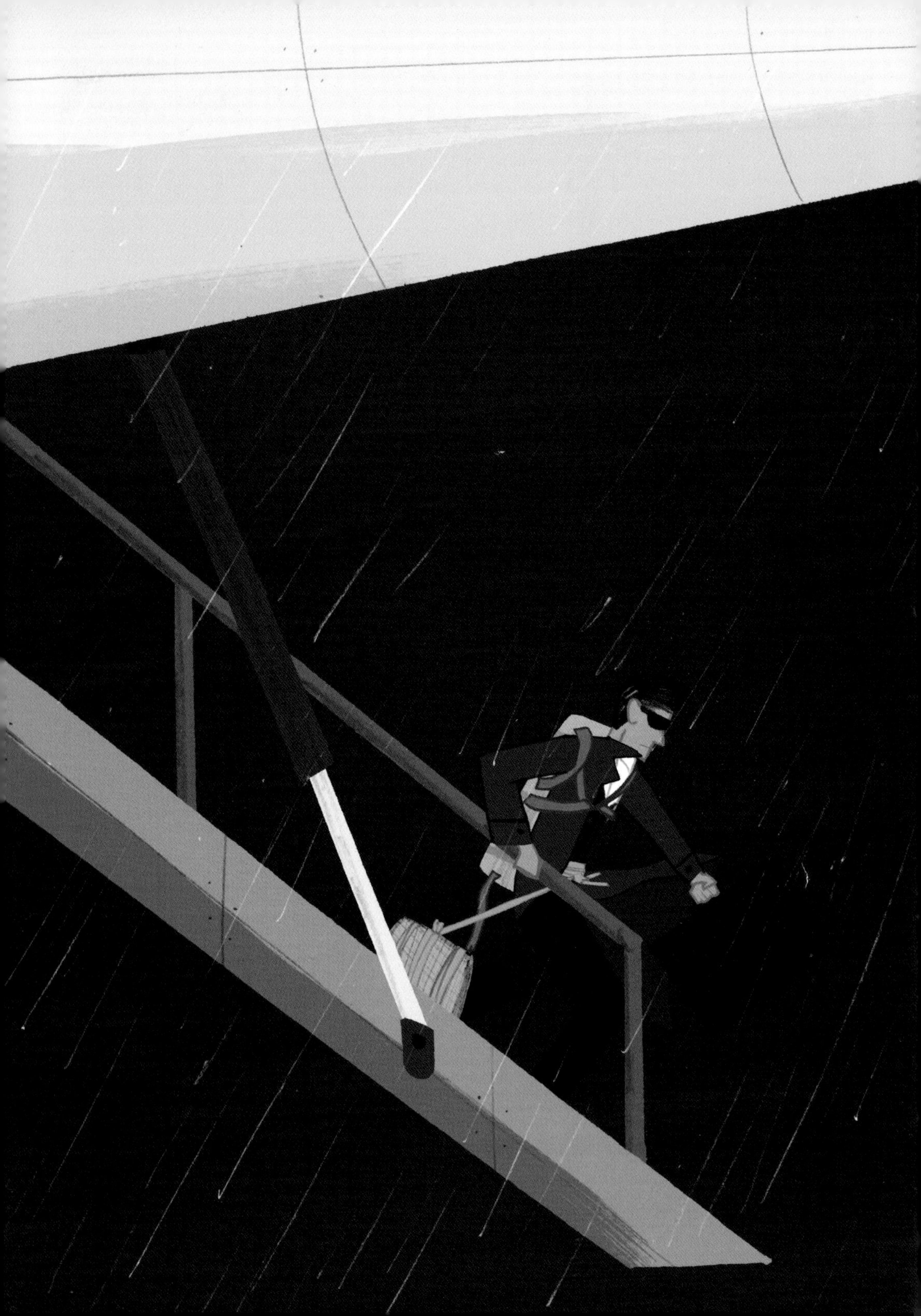

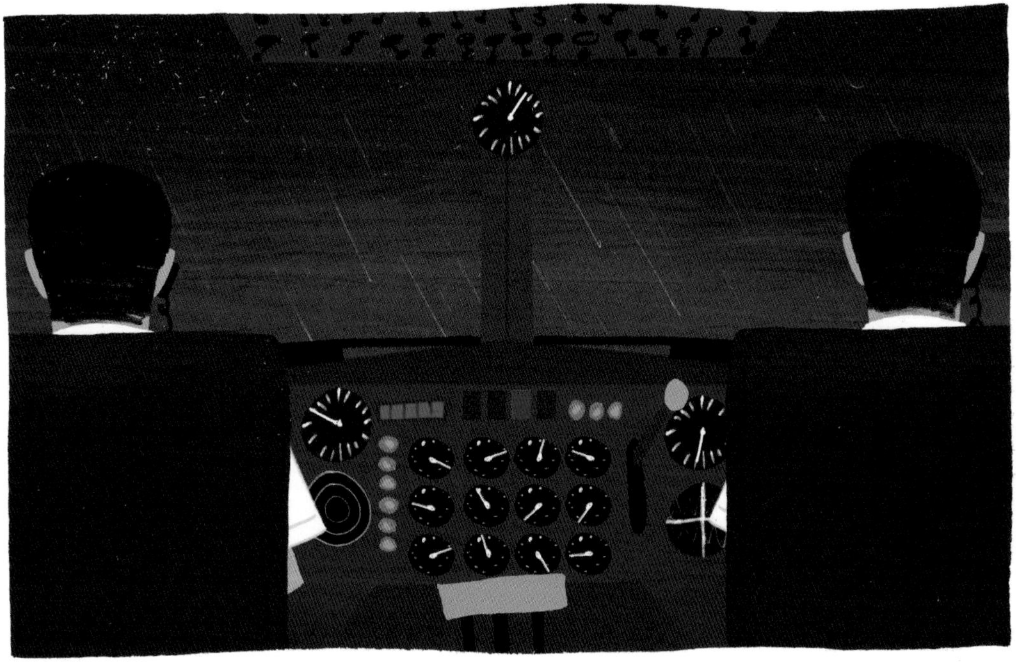

8:10 p.m.

The flight crew in the cockpit reported feeling a bump.

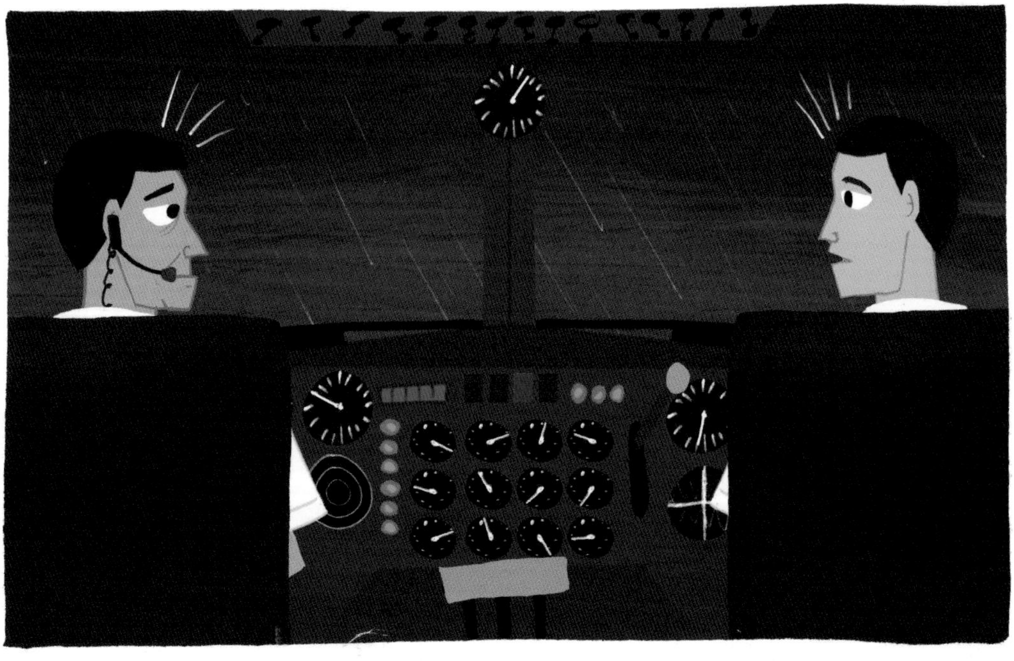

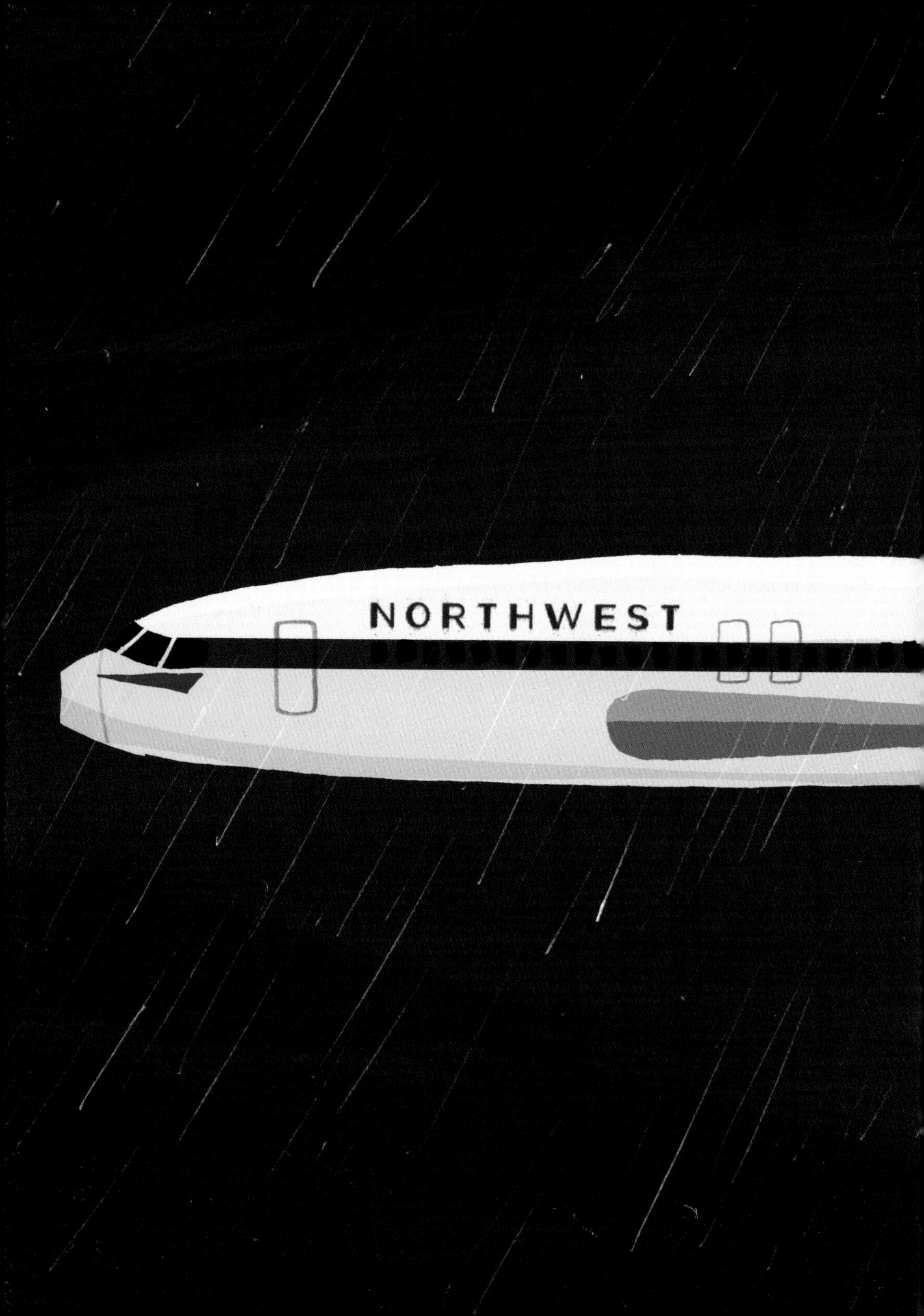
NORTHWEST

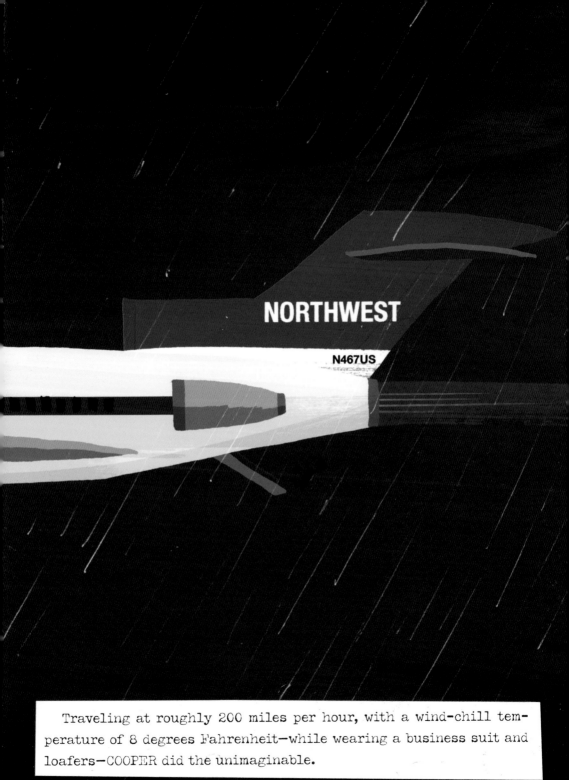

Traveling at roughly 200 miles per hour, with a wind-chill temperature of 8 degrees Fahrenheit—while wearing a business suit and loafers—COOPER did the unimaginable.

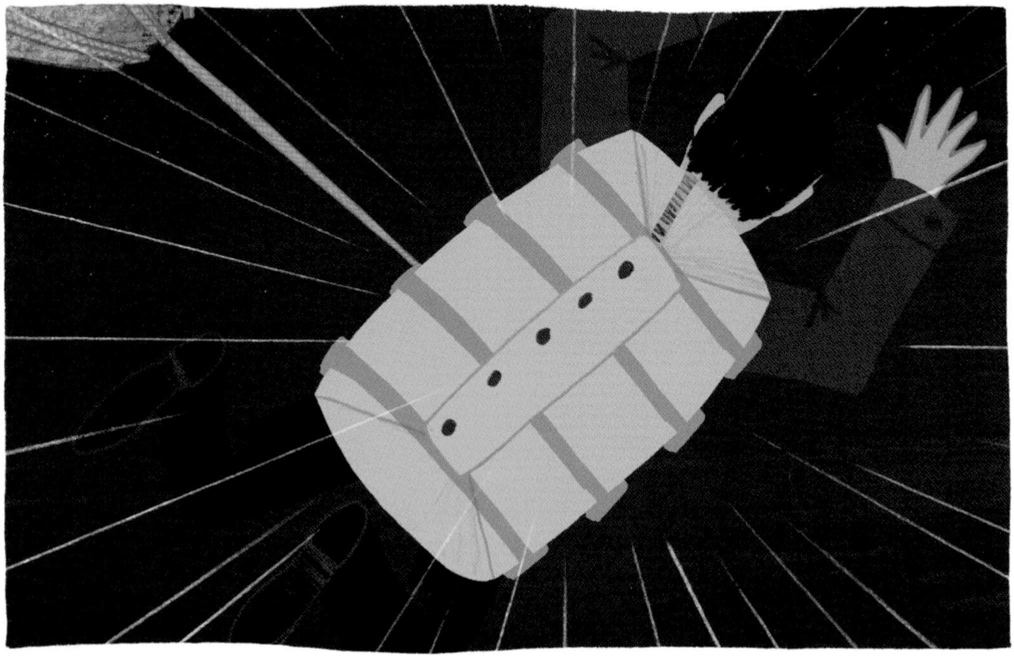

He leapt from the back of the airplane into the cold, wet night.

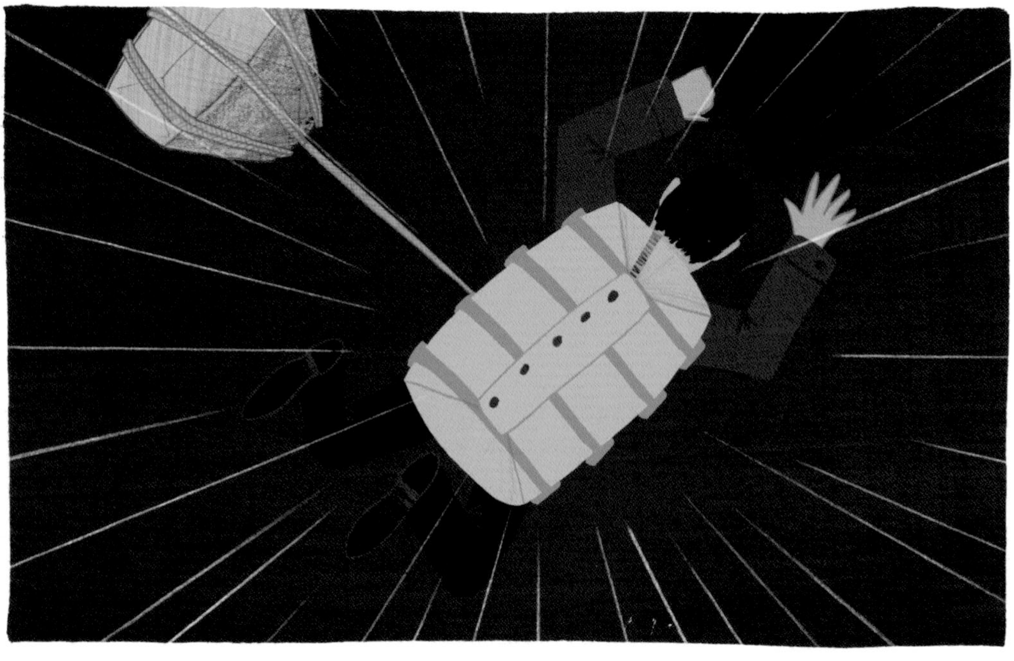

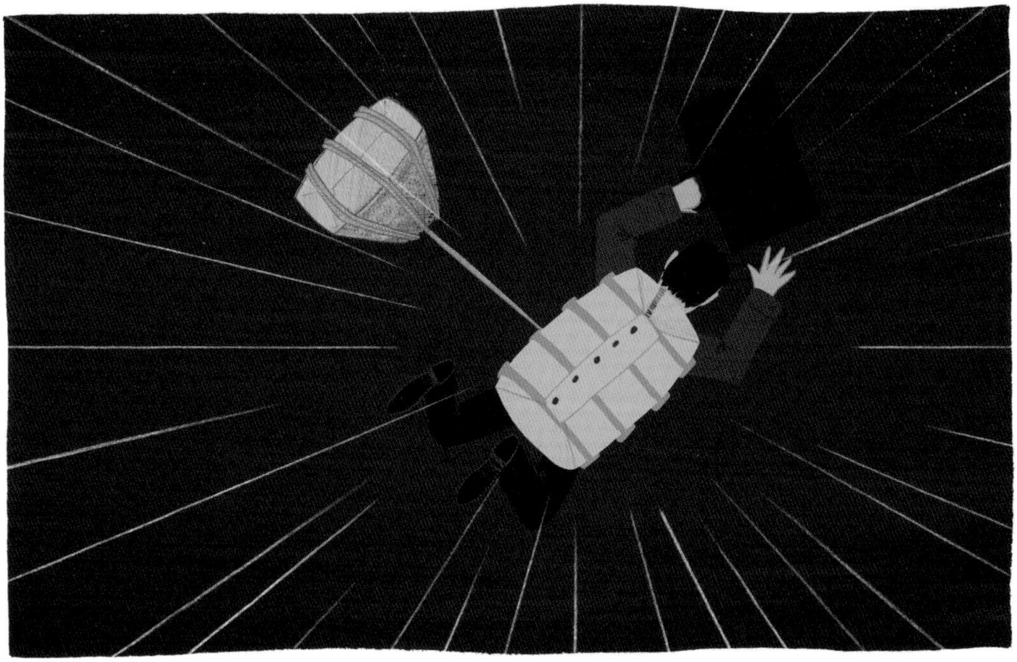

And plummeted to Earth somewhere over the forests of southern Washington.

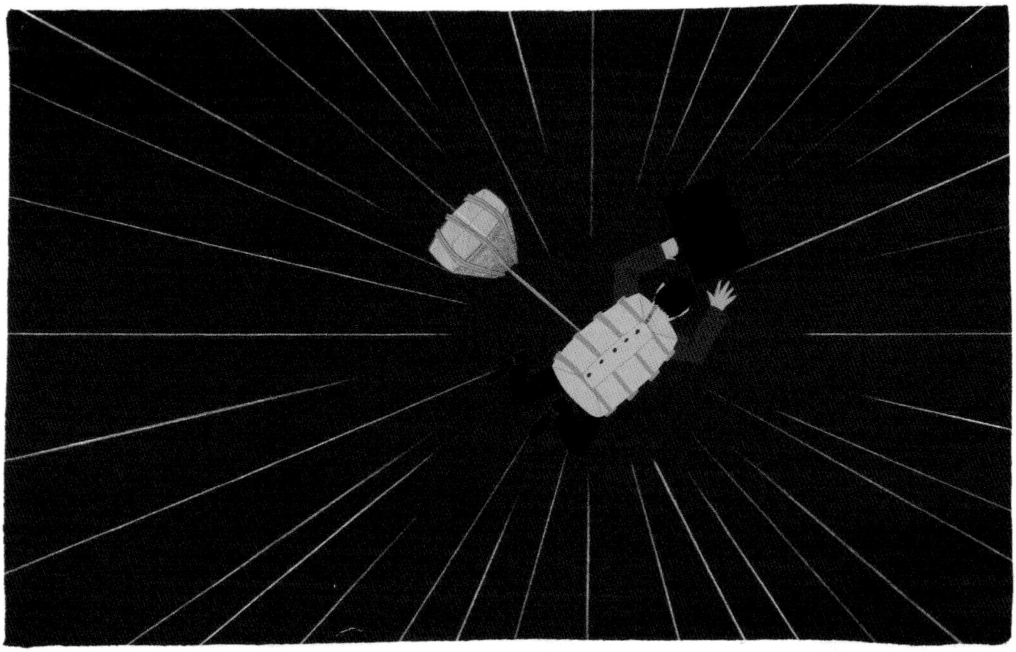

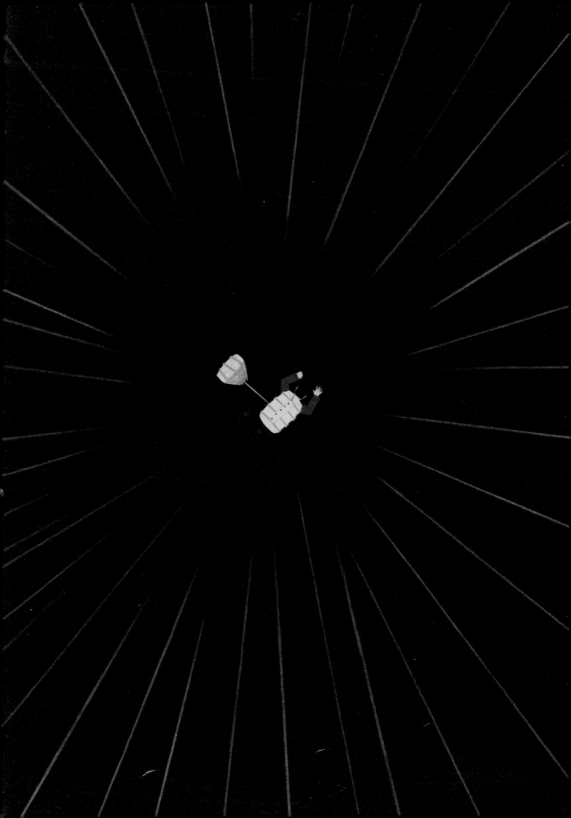

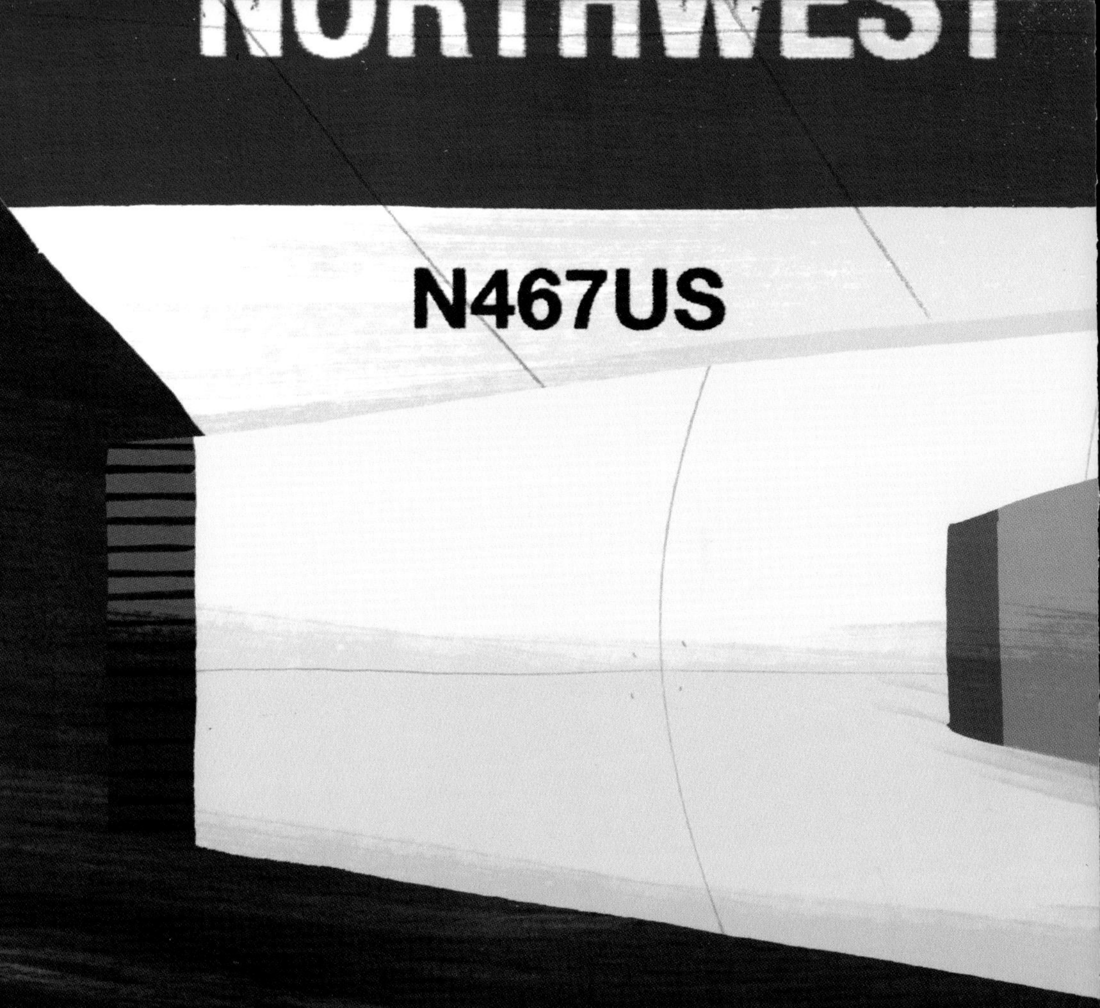
NORTHWEST
N467US

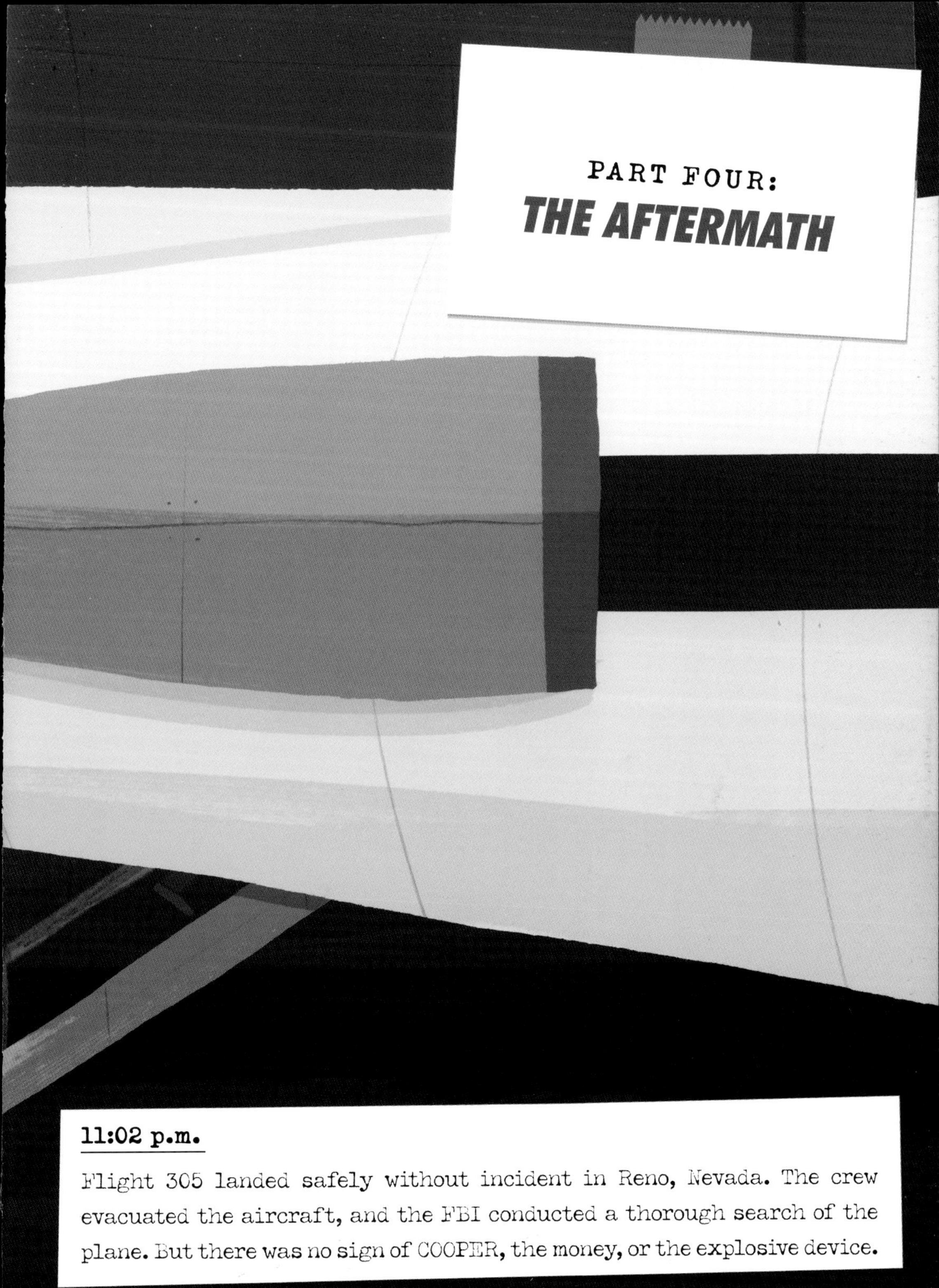

PART FOUR: THE AFTERMATH

11:02 p.m.

Flight 305 landed safely without incident in Reno, Nevada. The crew evacuated the aircraft, and the FBI conducted a thorough search of the plane. But there was no sign of COOPER, the money, or the explosive device.

COOPER took the original handwritten note that he had passed to Ms. SCHAFFNER with him, but he did happen to leave his plane ticket on board. And a partial fingerprint was recovered.

LATENT FINGERPRINT
EVIDENCE
DO NOT
TOUCH

PLANE TICKET

CLIP-ON NECKTIE

FINGERPRINT

COOPER also left his black JCPenney clip-on tie on a seat prior to jumping out of the plane. The FBI was able to collect a few strands of hair from the seat back, and seven Raleigh brand cigarette butts from the ashtray in seat 18-E. After extensive forensic examinations, DNA samples were recovered from the necktie and the hair.

DENCE
EAU OF INVESTIGATION

EVIDE
FEDERAL BUREAU O

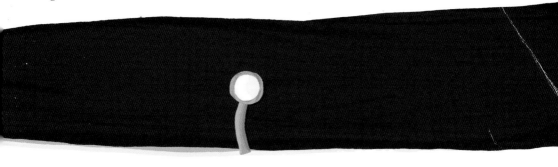

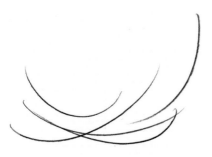

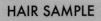

HAIR SAMPLE

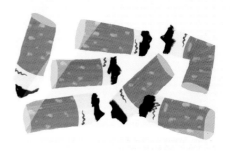

CIGARETTE BUTTS

A positive match for the fingerprint or DNA, however, has never been made.

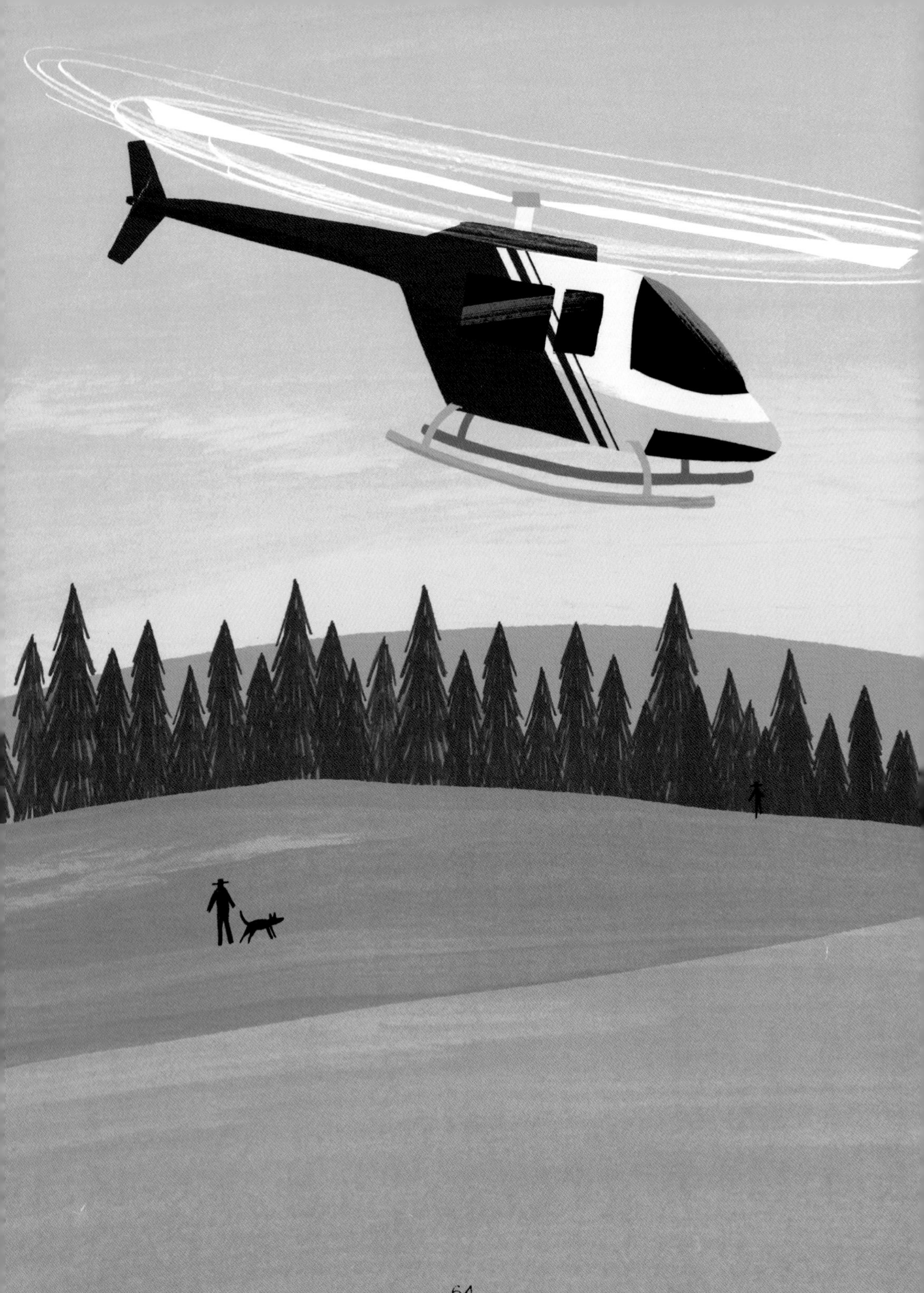

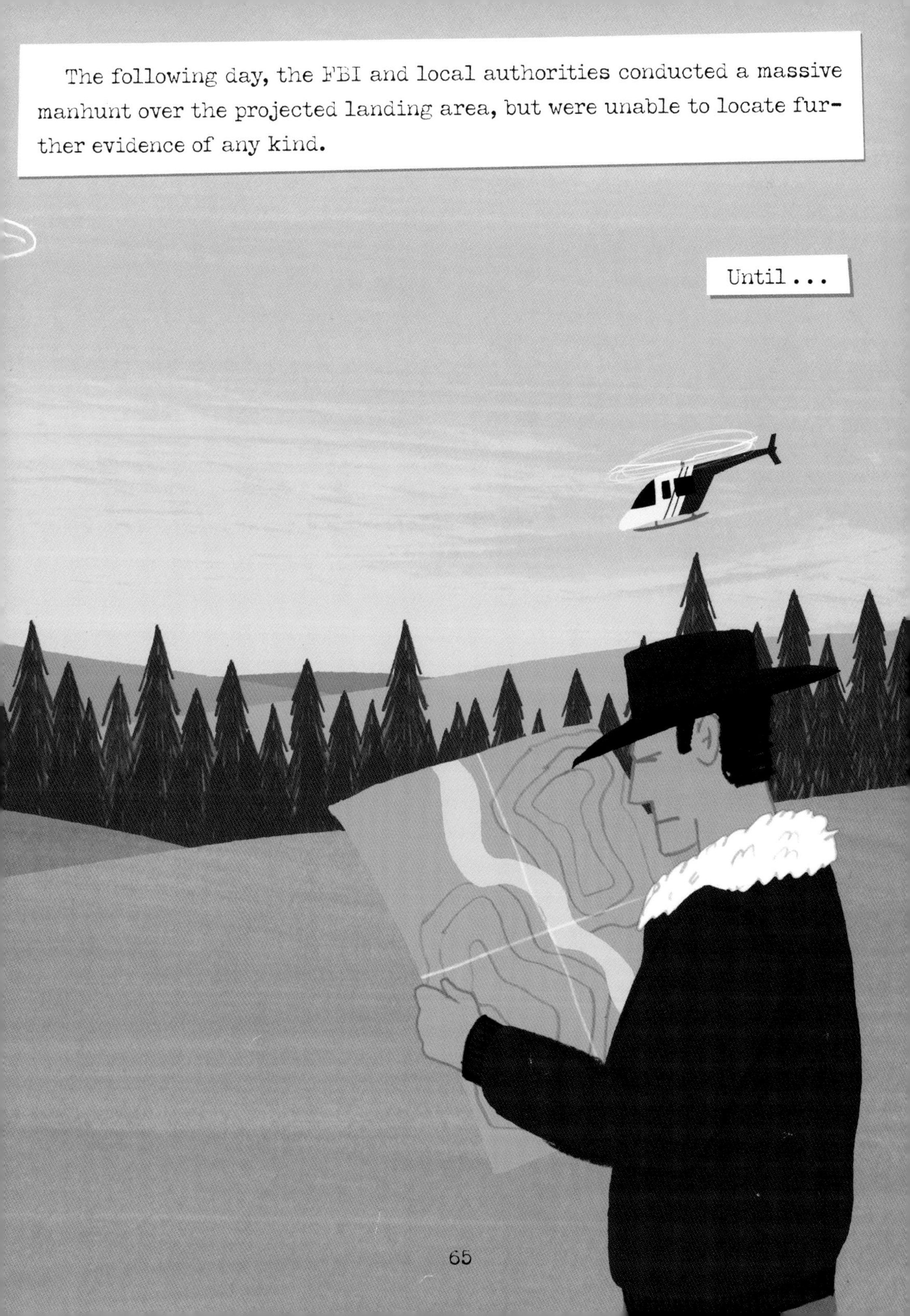
The following day, the FBI and local authorities conducted a massive manhunt over the projected landing area, but were unable to locate further evidence of any kind.
Until . . .

3,000 DAYS LATER.

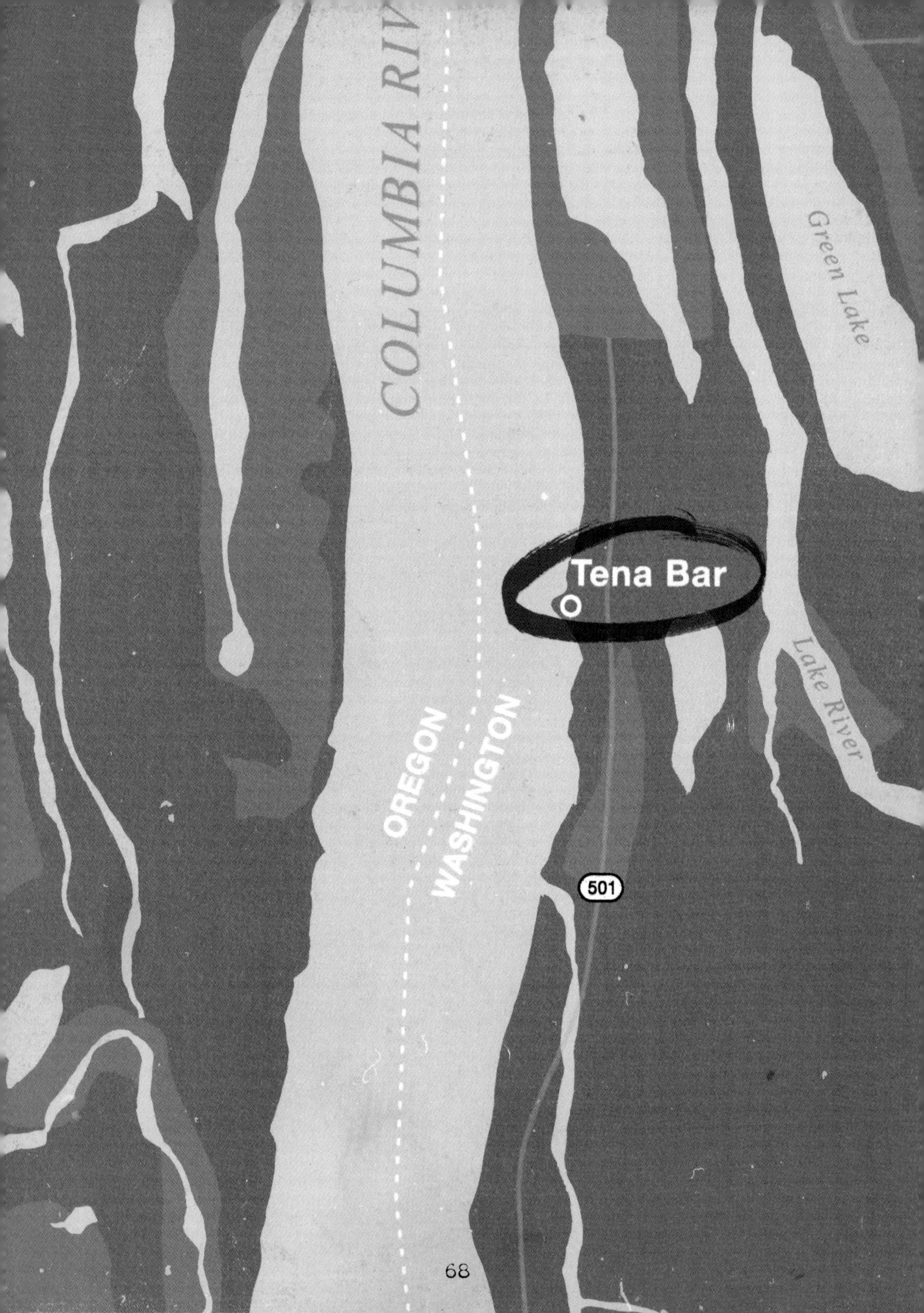
COLUMBIA RIV
Green Lake
Tena Bar
Lake River
OREGON
WASHINGTON
501

PART FIVE:

THE DISCOVERY

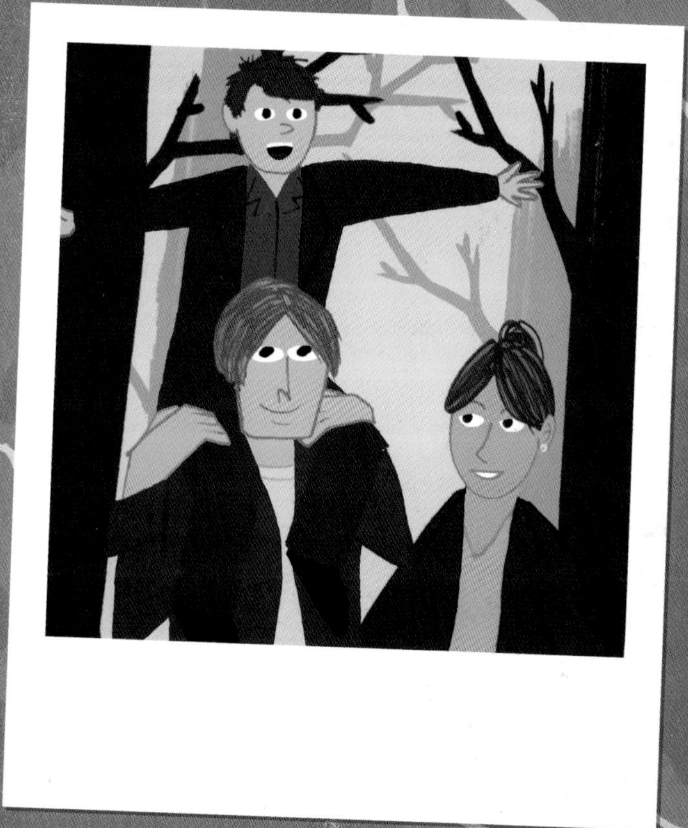

FEBRUARY 10, 1980

VANCOUVER, WASHINGTON

Eight-year-old BRIAN INGRAM was vacationing with his family on the banks of the COLUMBIA RIVER in the TENA BAR area.

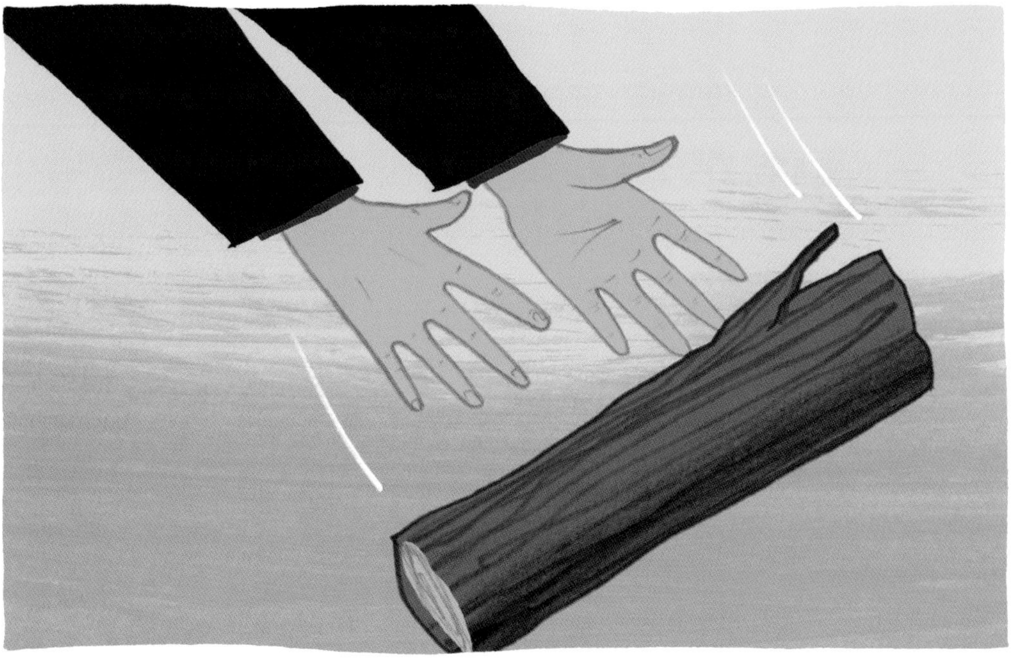

It was around lunchtime when BRIAN decided to build a campfire. After gathering some wood, he was clearing an area when he felt something odd in the sand.

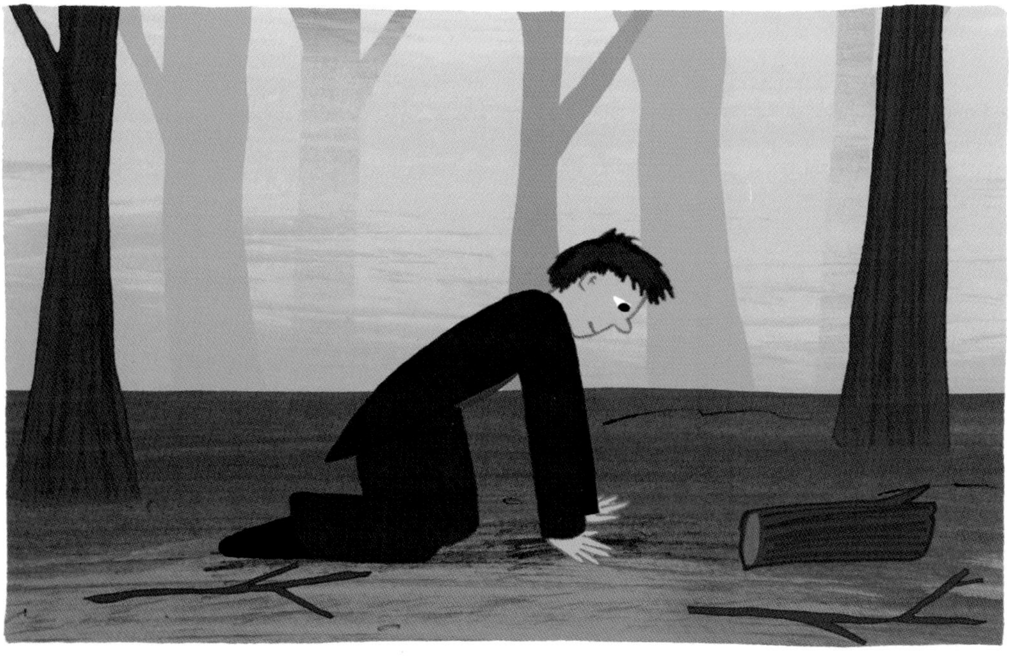

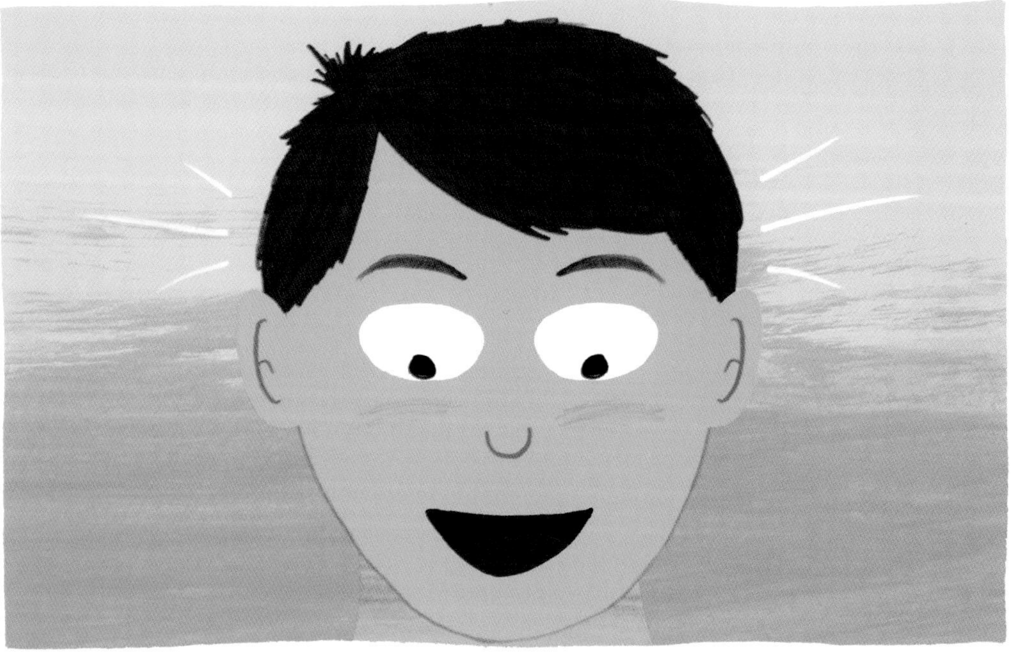

BRIAN brushed the earth aside, and staring right back up at him through the soil was our seventh president, Andrew Jackson.

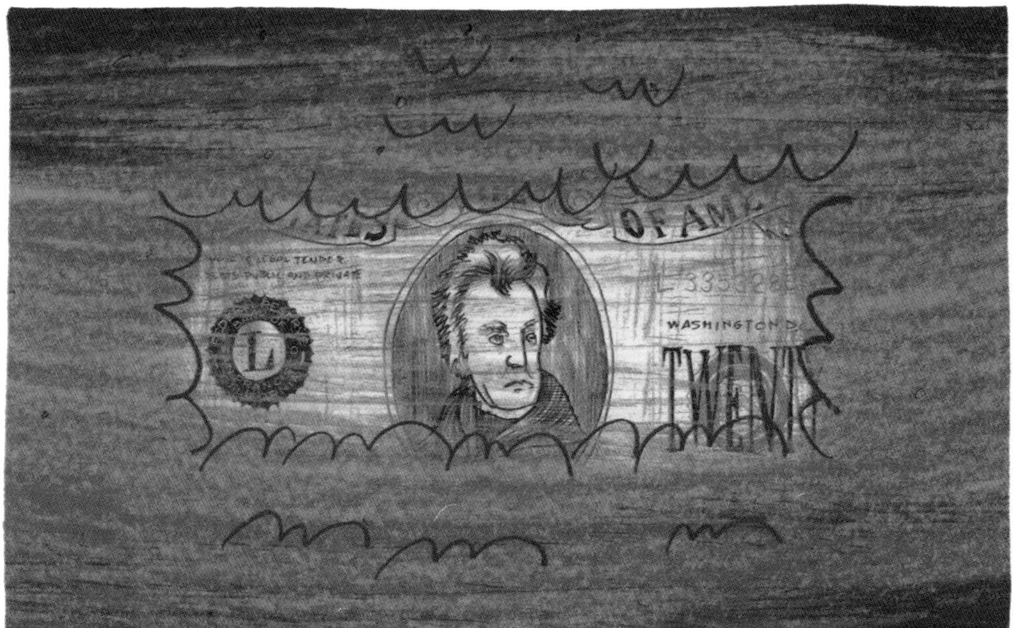

Unbelievably, sitting there barely below the surface were three moldy, decaying bundles of twenty-dollar bills, totaling $5,800 in all. And just like that—with a serendipitous stroke of luck—a boy who happened to be in the right place at the right time made the first break in the case in over eight years.

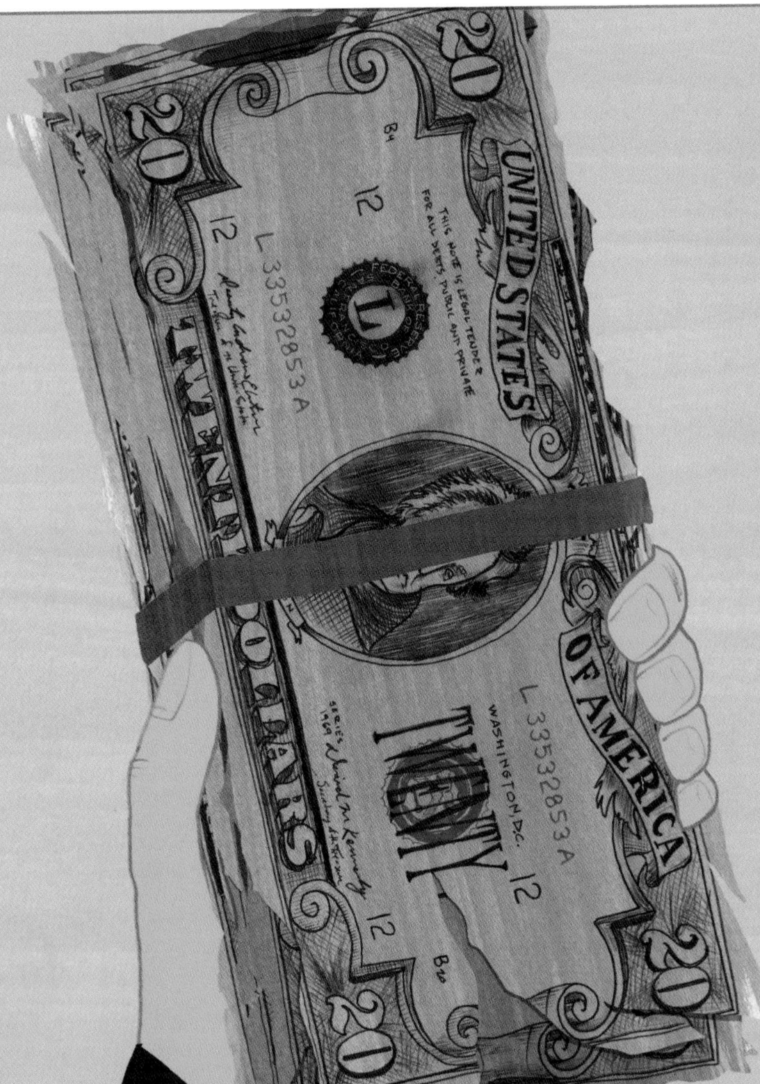
UNITED STATES
OF AMERICA
THIS NOTE IS LEGAL TENDER FOR ALL DEBTS, PUBLIC AND PRIVATE
L 33532853 A
WASHINGTON, D.C.
TWENTY
20

The FBI was notified, and they were able to confirm that the serial numbers were a match for COOPER'S ransom money.

The next day, a team of federal agents and local police officers dug up the entire beach, but they were unable to locate any other evidence. Despite reigniting public interest in the case, no further trace of DAN COOPER, his parachute, or the money has ever been found.

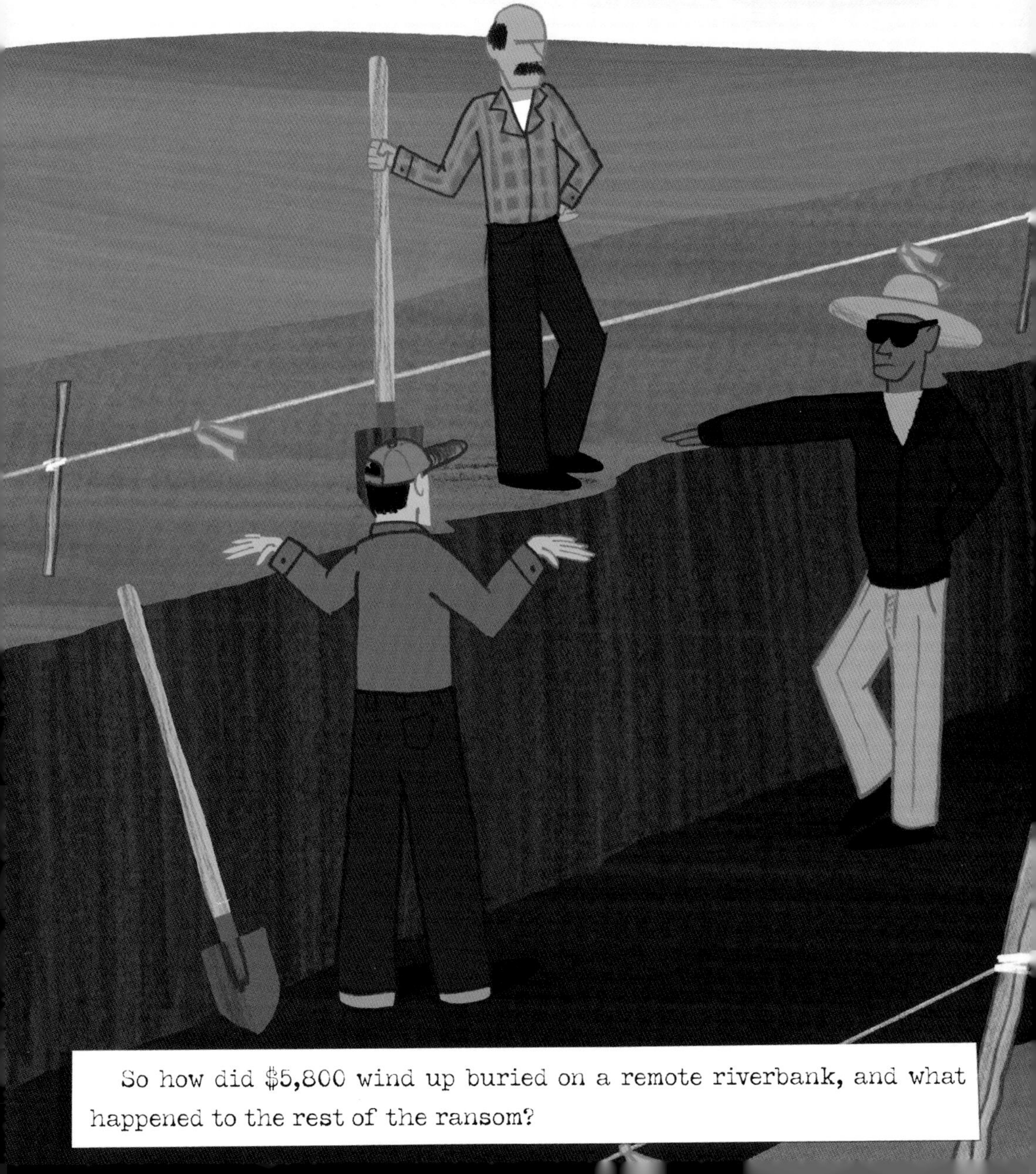

So how did $5,800 wind up buried on a remote riverbank, and what happened to the rest of the ransom?

One popular theory was that the bills wound up buried on the shore of the river after a dredging operation that had taken place in 1974.

According to the FBI's files, though, the dredge used in 1974 was only 24 inches in diameter, making it nearly impossible for three wads of paper to be able to pass through it without being completely shredded.

And if the money had been buried in the sand prior to the dredging operation, it would have been several feet underground, rather than just below the surface.

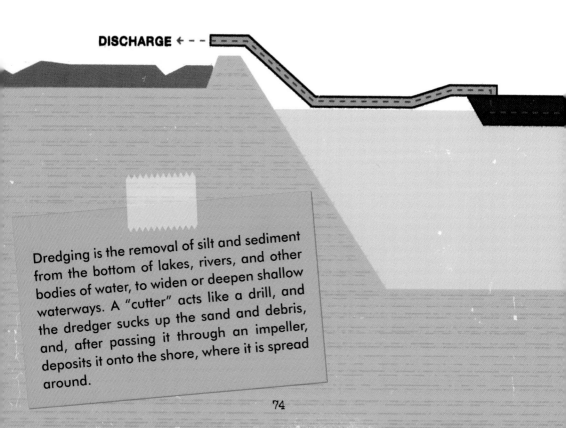

DISCHARGE ← − −

Dredging is the removal of silt and sediment from the bottom of lakes, rivers, and other bodies of water, to widen or deepen shallow waterways. A "cutter" acts like a drill, and the dredger sucks up the sand and debris, and, after passing it through an impeller, deposits it onto the shore, where it is spread around.

Centrifugal Pump

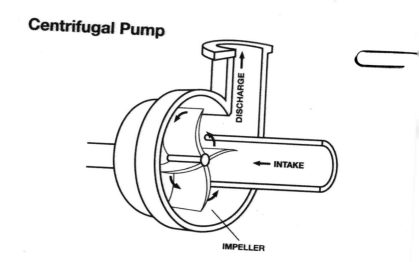

DISCHARGE

INTAKE

IMPELLER

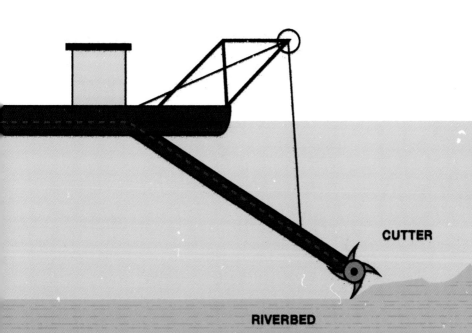

CUTTER

RIVERBED

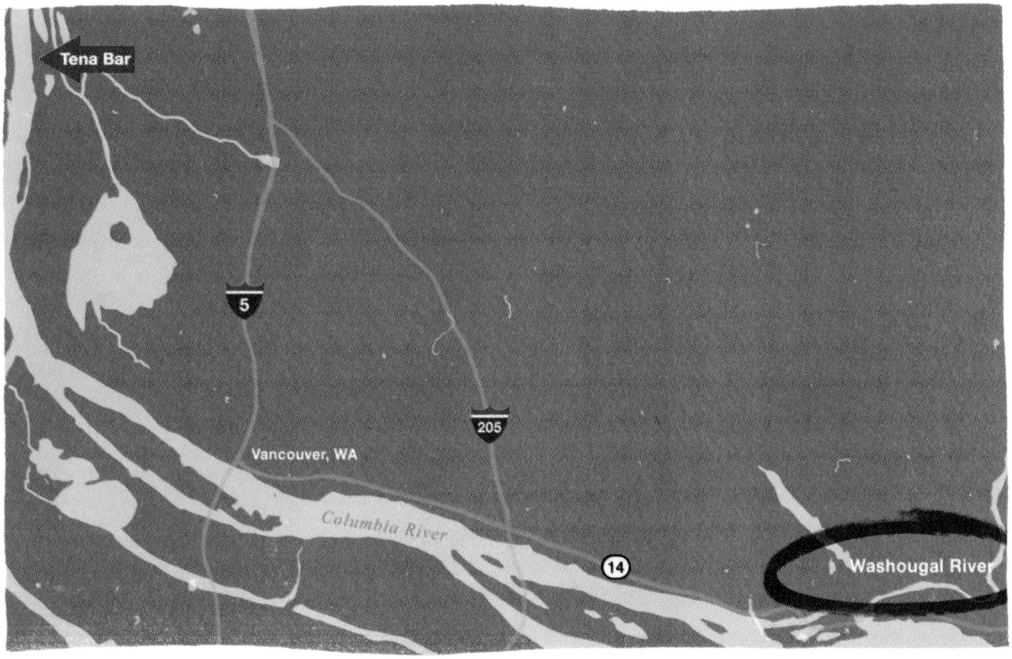
Tena Bar
5
205
Vancouver, WA
Columbia River
14
Washougal River

Another popular idea was the "Washougal Washdown Theory," which hypothesized that the bank bag somehow landed in the WASHOUGAL RIVER and spent the next several years slowly washing downstream.

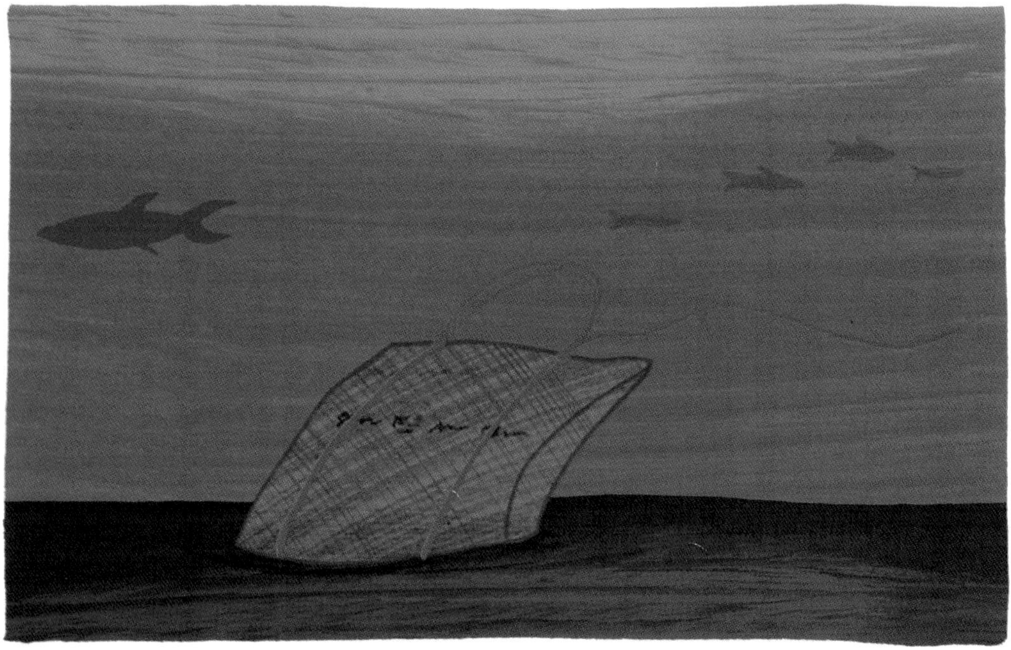

The canvas bag would have taken the brunt of Mother Nature's force, but at some point, the three bundles of cash must have become dislodged and floated up onshore after the dredging operation in 1974, where they were then buried for the next several years.

Though it sounds plausible, this theory has also been scientifically ruled out. For starters, Flight 305 would have had to fly about 20 miles east of where the flight path data places it in order for the money to fall into the Washougal River. And studies completed with the same rubber bands that were found wrapped around the bundles of money showed that they deteriorated within a year of being submerged in the murky water, and in no way could have survived several waterlogged years.

In some ways, the mystery of how $5,800 wound up on that beach is as great a mystery as the identity of D.B. COOPER himself.

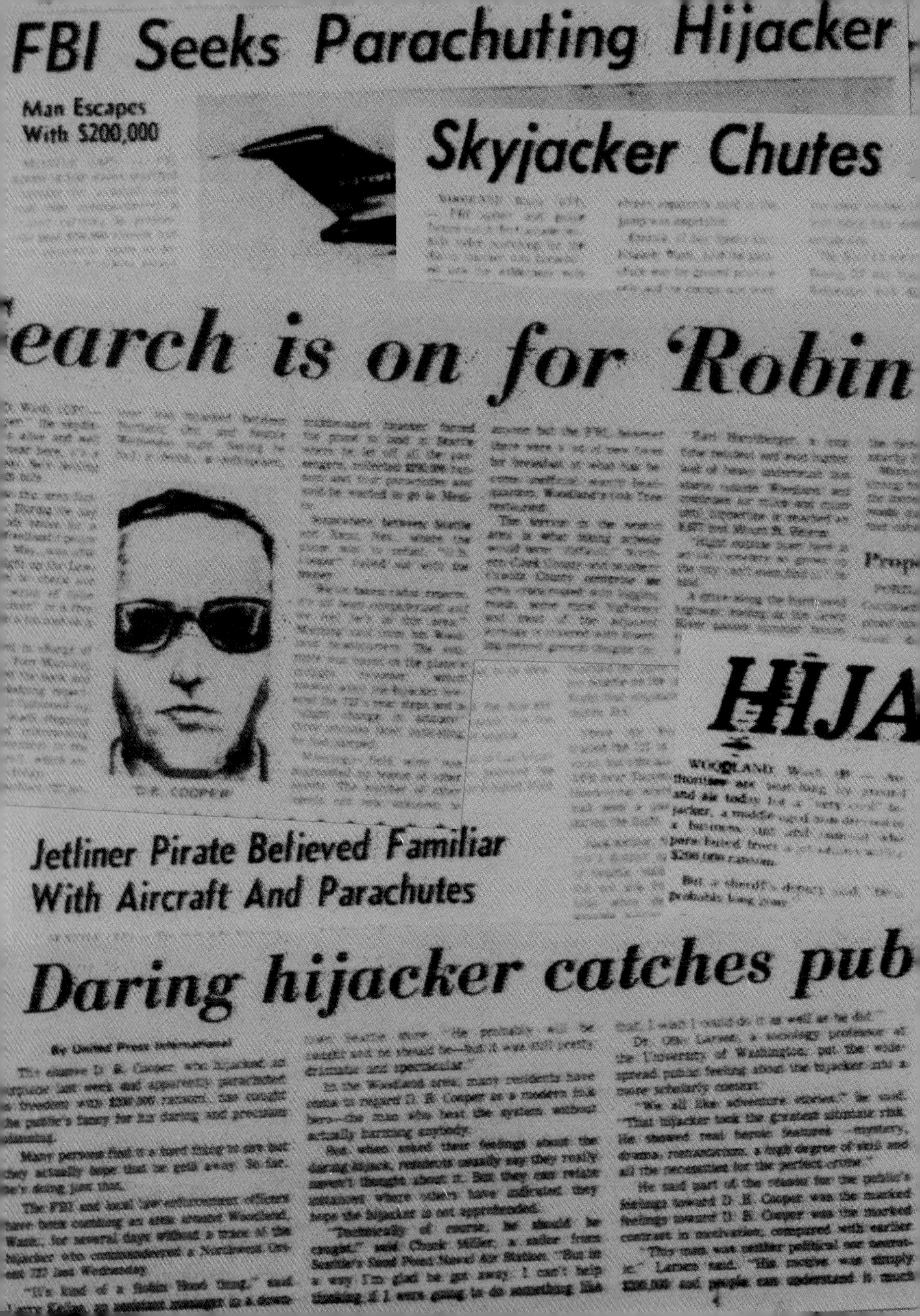

FBI Seeks Parachuting Hijacker

Man Escapes With $200,000

Skyjacker Chutes

WOODLAND, Wash. (UPI) — FBI agents and police hammered the backwoods hillsides searching for the daring hijacker who bailed out into the wilderness with...

earch is on for 'Robin

D. B. COOPER

Jetliner Pirate Believed Familiar With Aircraft And Parachutes

HIJA

WOODLAND, Wash. —

Daring hijacker catches pub

By United Press International

The elusive D. B. Cooper who hijacked an airplane last week and apparently parachuted to freedom with $200,000 ransom, has caught the public's fancy for his daring and precision planning.

Many persons find it a hard thing to say but they actually hope that he gets away. So far, he's doing just that.

The FBI and local law enforcement officers have been combing an area around Woodland, Wash., for several days without a trace of the hijacker who commandeered a Northwest Orient 727 last Wednesday.

"It's kind of a Robin Hood thing," said Larry Kline, an assistant manager in a down-

town Seattle store. "He probably will be caught and he should be—but it was still pretty dramatic and spectacular."

In the Woodland area, many residents have come to regard D. B. Cooper as a modern folk hero—the man who beat the system without actually harming anybody.

But, when asked their feelings about the daring hijack, residents usually say they really haven't thought about it. But they can relate instances where others have indicated they hope the hijacker is not apprehended.

"Technically, of course, he should be caught," said Chuck Miller, a sailor from Seattle's Sand Point Naval Air Station. "But in a way I'm glad he got away. I can't help thinking if I were going to do something like

that, I wish I could do it as well as he did."

Dr. Otto Larsen, a sociology professor at the University of Washington, put the widespread public feeling about the hijacker into a more scholarly context.

"We all like adventure stories," he said. "That hijacker took the greatest ultimate risk. He showed real heroic features — mystery, drama, romanticism, a high degree of skill and all the necessities for the perfect crime."

He said part of the reason for the public's feelings toward D. B. Cooper was the marked contrast in motivation, compared with earlier hijackings.

"This man was neither political nor terroristic," Larsen said. "His motive was simply $200,000 and people can understand it more

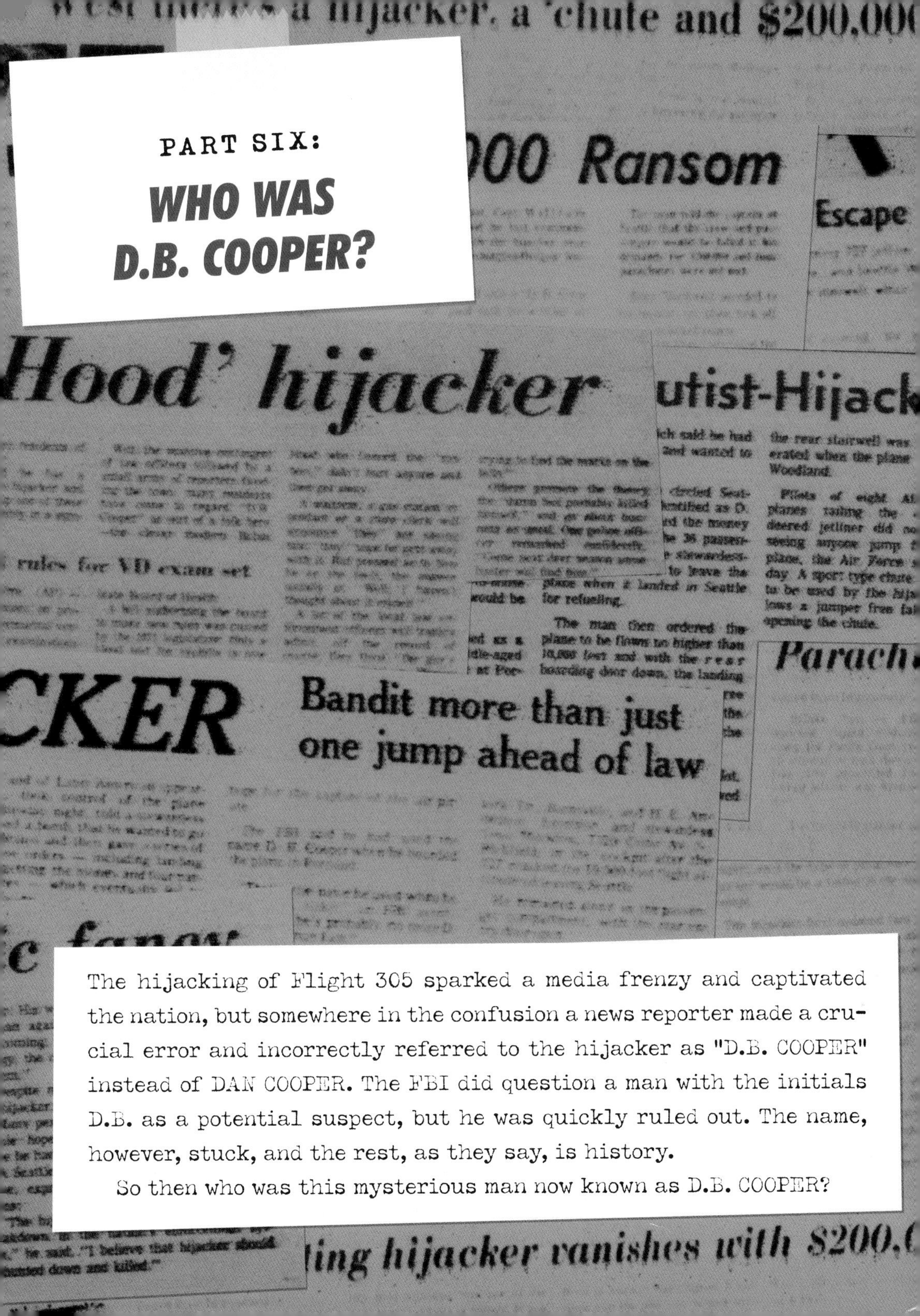
000 Ransom
Escape
Hood' hijacker
utist-Hijack
rules for VD exam set
CKER
Bandit more than just one jump ahead of law
ing hijacker vanishes with $200,

PART SIX:

WHO WAS D.B. COOPER?

The hijacking of Flight 305 sparked a media frenzy and captivated the nation, but somewhere in the confusion a news reporter made a crucial error and incorrectly referred to the hijacker as "D.B. COOPER" instead of DAN COOPER. The FBI did question a man with the initials D.B. as a potential suspect, but he was quickly ruled out. The name, however, stuck, and the rest, as they say, is history.

So then who was this mysterious man now known as D.B. COOPER?

Over the years, the FBI considered hundreds of possible suspects, but none were as compelling as RICHARD FLOYD MCCOY JR.

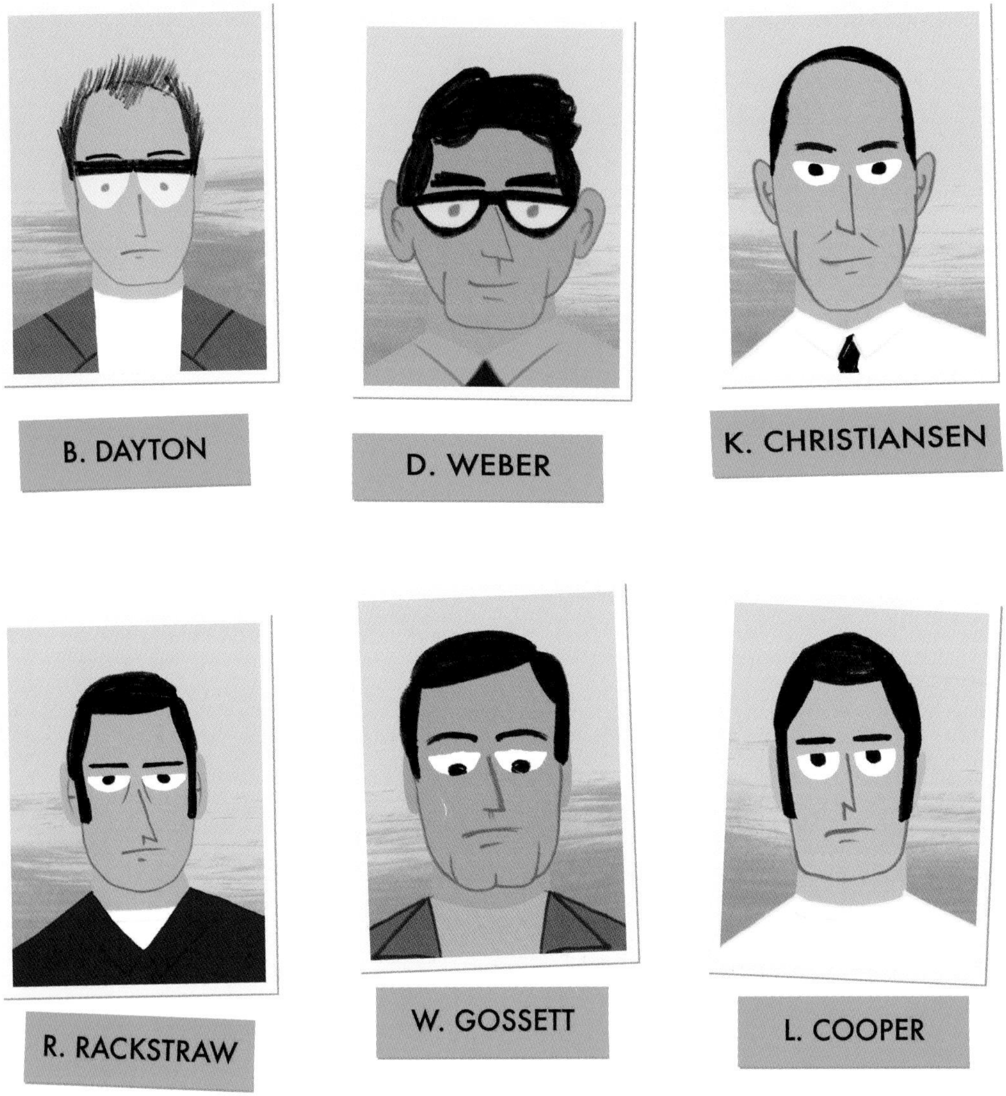
B. DAYTON
D. WEBER
K. CHRISTIANSEN
R. RACKSTRAW
W. GOSSETT
L. COOPER

CRIMINAL REPORT

NAME: RICHARD FLOYD McCOY, JR.

DOB: DECEMBER 7, 1942

CRIME: AIRCRAFT PIRACY

STATUS: DECEASED

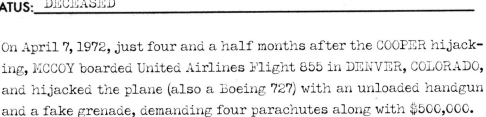

On April 7, 1972, just four and a half months after the COOPER hijacking, MCCOY boarded United Airlines Flight 855 in DENVER, COLORADO, and hijacked the plane (also a Boeing 727) with an unloaded handgun and a fake grenade, demanding four parachutes along with $500,000.

After delivery of the money and the parachutes in SAN FRANCISCO, Flight 855 took off, and MCCOY leapt from the rear staircase somewhere over PROVO, UTAH.

Two days later, MCCOY was apprehended with the ransom money in his possession. He was tried, convicted, and sentenced to forty-five years in prison.

In 1974 he escaped by crashing a garbage truck through the penitentiary's main gate in LEWISBURG, PENNSYLVANIA. Three months later, he was killed in a shootout with FBI agents in VIRGINIA BEACH.

While many believe—due to the overwhelming similarities in the two cases—that MCCOY was in fact D.B. COOPER, the FBI has refuted that suspicion based on the age discrepancy (MCCOY was only twenty-eight in 1971, rather than in his forties). Additionally, witnesses placed MCCOY at his home in Utah on Thanksgiving Day.

UNITED STATES DEPARTMENT OF JUSTICE

FEDERAL BUREAU OF INVESTIGATION

WASHINGTON, DC

There is another theory, popularized by FBI SPECIAL AGENT LARRY CARR, that proposes COOPER was of French Canadian origin. Both TINA MUCKLOW and FLORENCE SCHAFFNER have stated that the hijacker had no distinguishable accent, and they both assumed he was possibly from the Midwest. However, while communicating with the pilot, COOPER used the term "NEGOTIABLE AMERICAN CURRENCY," which doesn't sound like a phrase that a native-born American would ever use.

Furthermore, it was discovered that DAN COOPER was the name of a French comic book character who was a fighter pilot in the Royal Canadian Air Force. At the time, the comic series, anthologized in TINTIN magazine, had never been translated into English.

This, along with COOPER'S familiarity with the Boeing 727, led AGENT CARR to theorize that COOPER had served in the air force somewhere in Europe and become acquainted with the Dan Cooper comic books.

AGENT CARR

EX-11

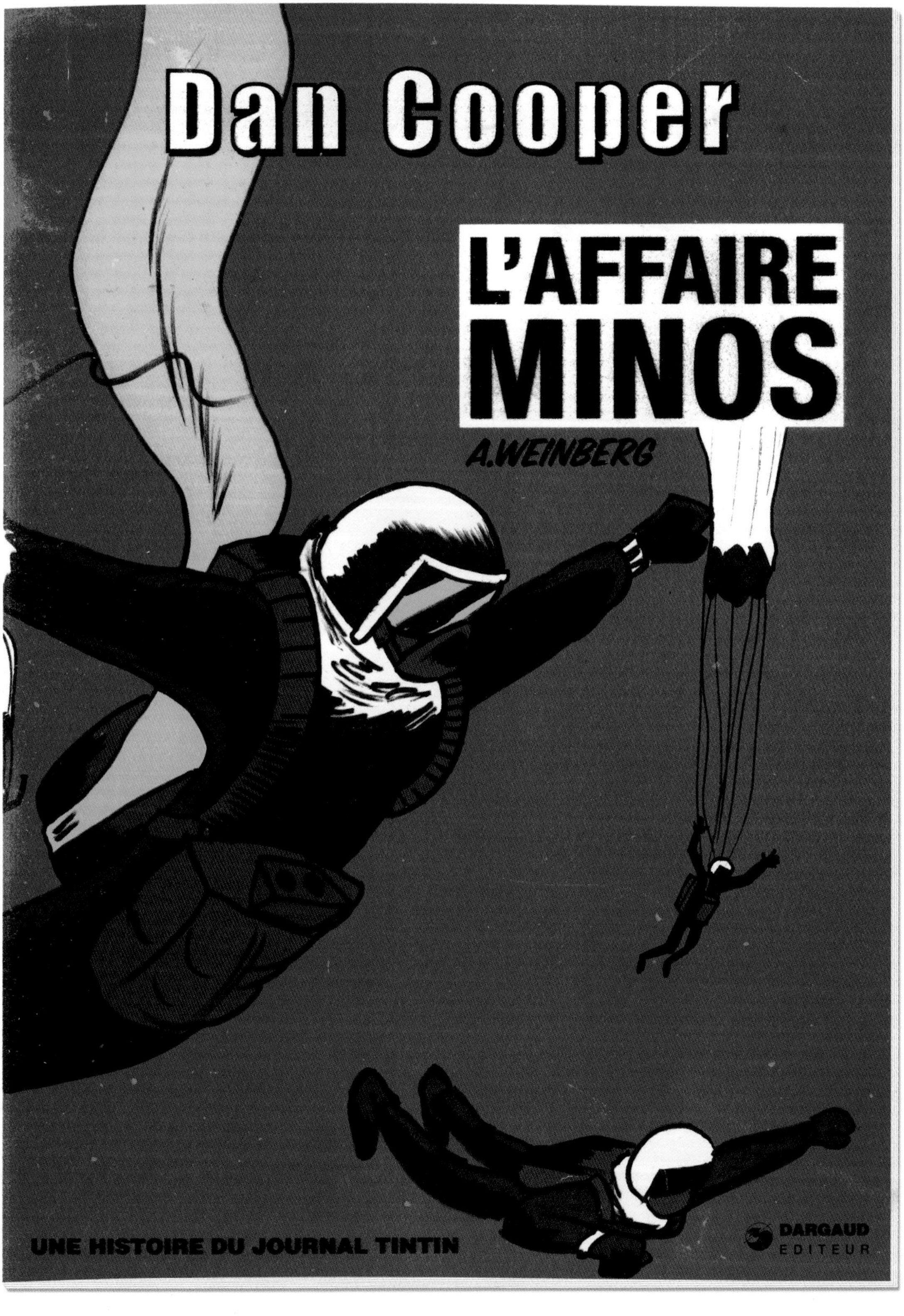

Dan Cooper
L'AFFAIRE MINOS
A.WEINBERG
UNE HISTOIRE DU JOURNAL TINTIN
DARGAUD EDITEUR

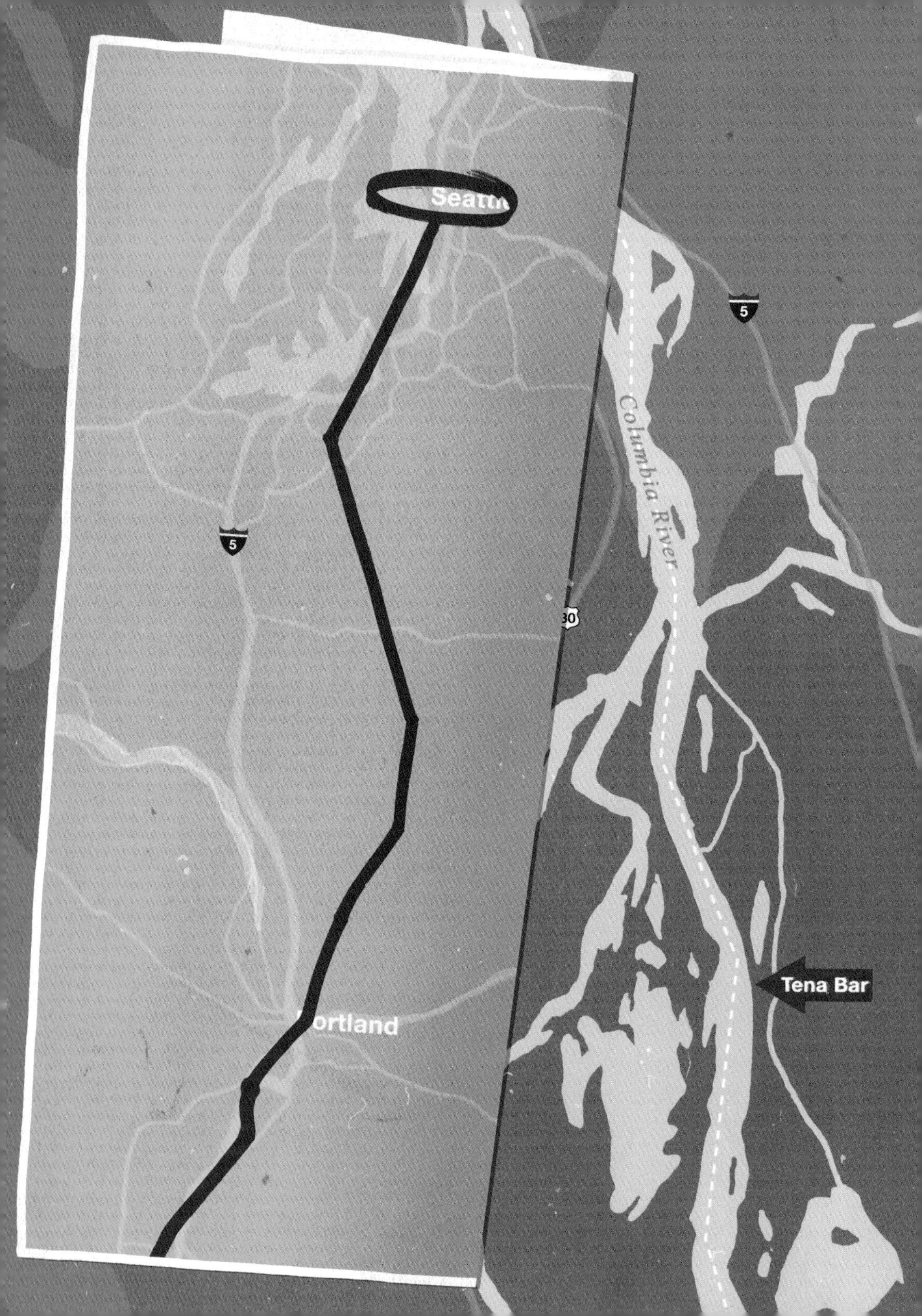
Seattle
5
Portland
5
30
Columbia River
Tena Bar

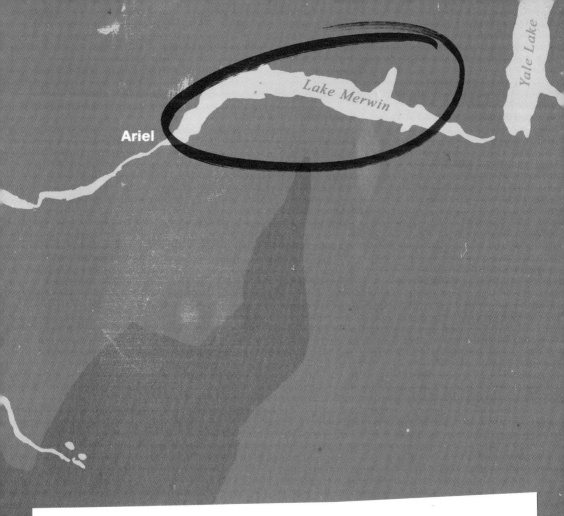

Ariel

Lake Merwin

Yale Lake

Using flight path data and communication transcripts, it is estimated that COOPER'S projected landing area was near ARIEL, WASHINGTON, with a strong possibility that he descended smack-dab into the middle of LAKE MERWIN.

In all likelihood he perished on that fateful evening in 1971, but the FBI's Underwater Evidence Collection Team was unable to locate a body, a fragment of a parachute, or any physical evidence whatsoever.

To further add to the mystery, there were no missing persons reported in the weeks leading up to and following the hijacking who fit the suspect's description.

It's almost as if he vanished into thin air.

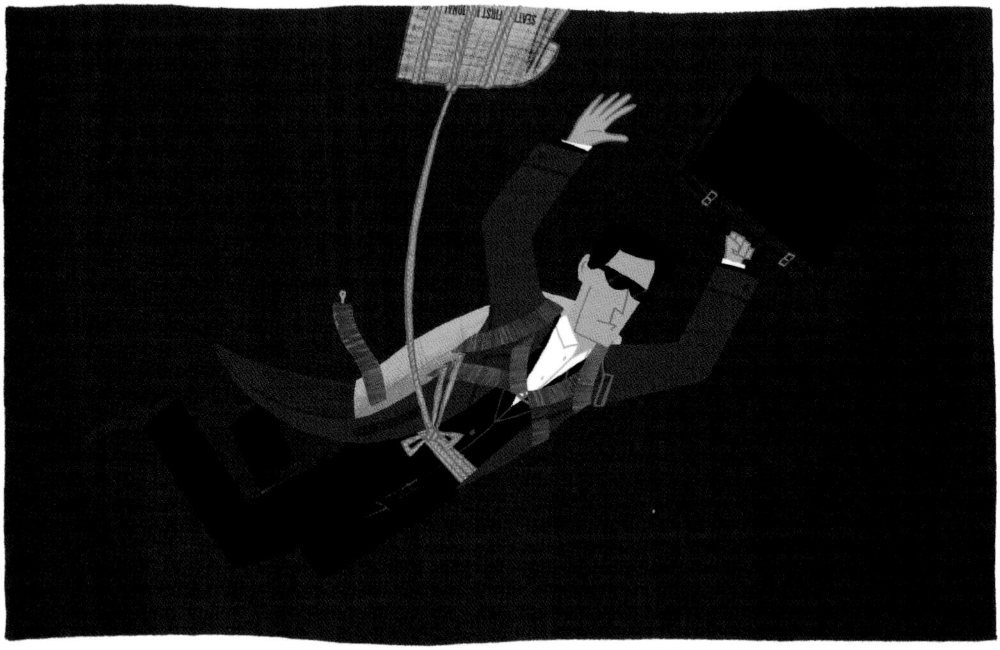

If COOPER somehow managed to miraculously survive the terrifying ordeal of hurling himself out the back of an airplane and parachuting into the pitch black—

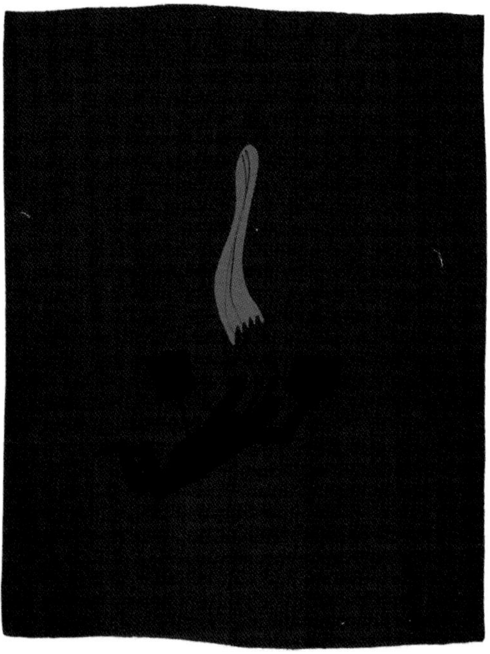

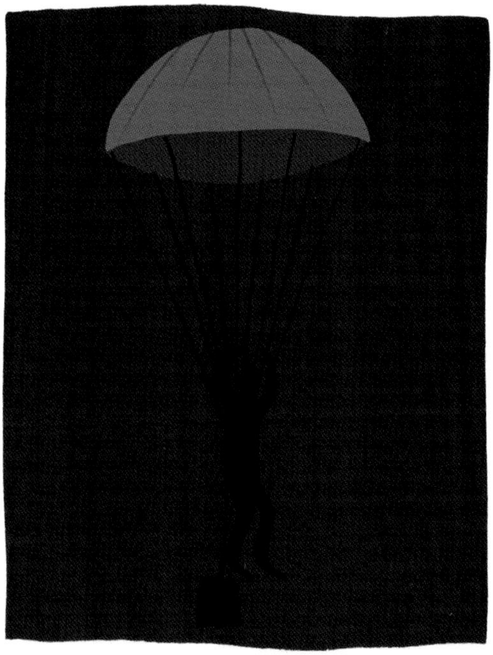

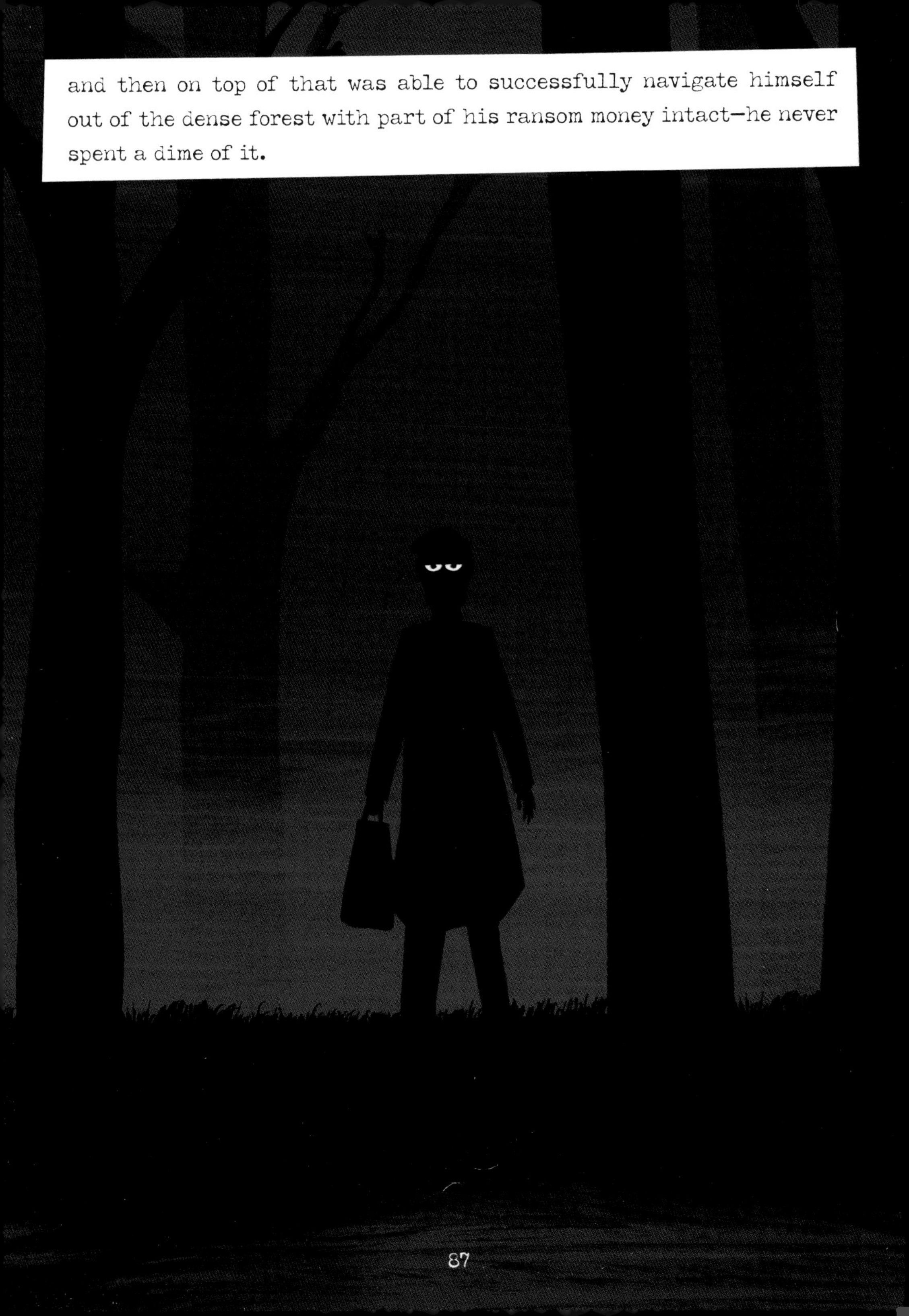
and then on top of that was able to successfully navigate himself out of the dense forest with part of his ransom money intact—he never spent a dime of it.

It's not known whether COOPER perished that evening, or how some of the money turned up on a remote riverbank eight years later. The only thing we do know for certain is that $194,200 remains unaccounted for somewhere out there in the Pacific Northwest, and it's just waiting to be found.

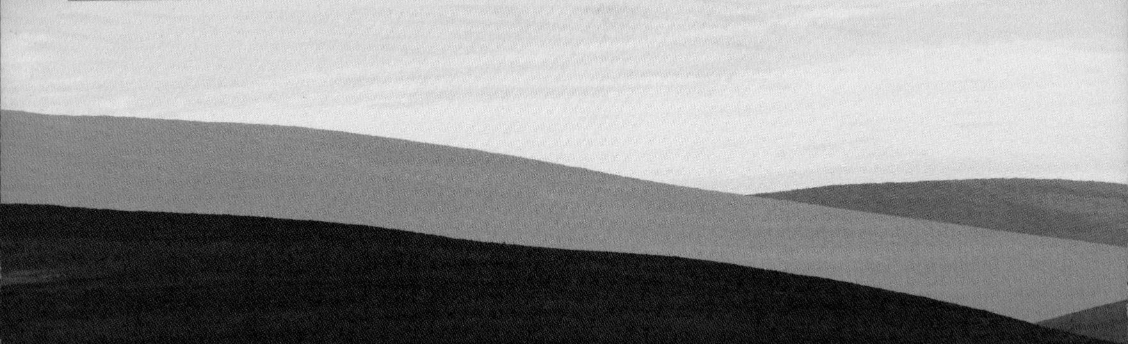

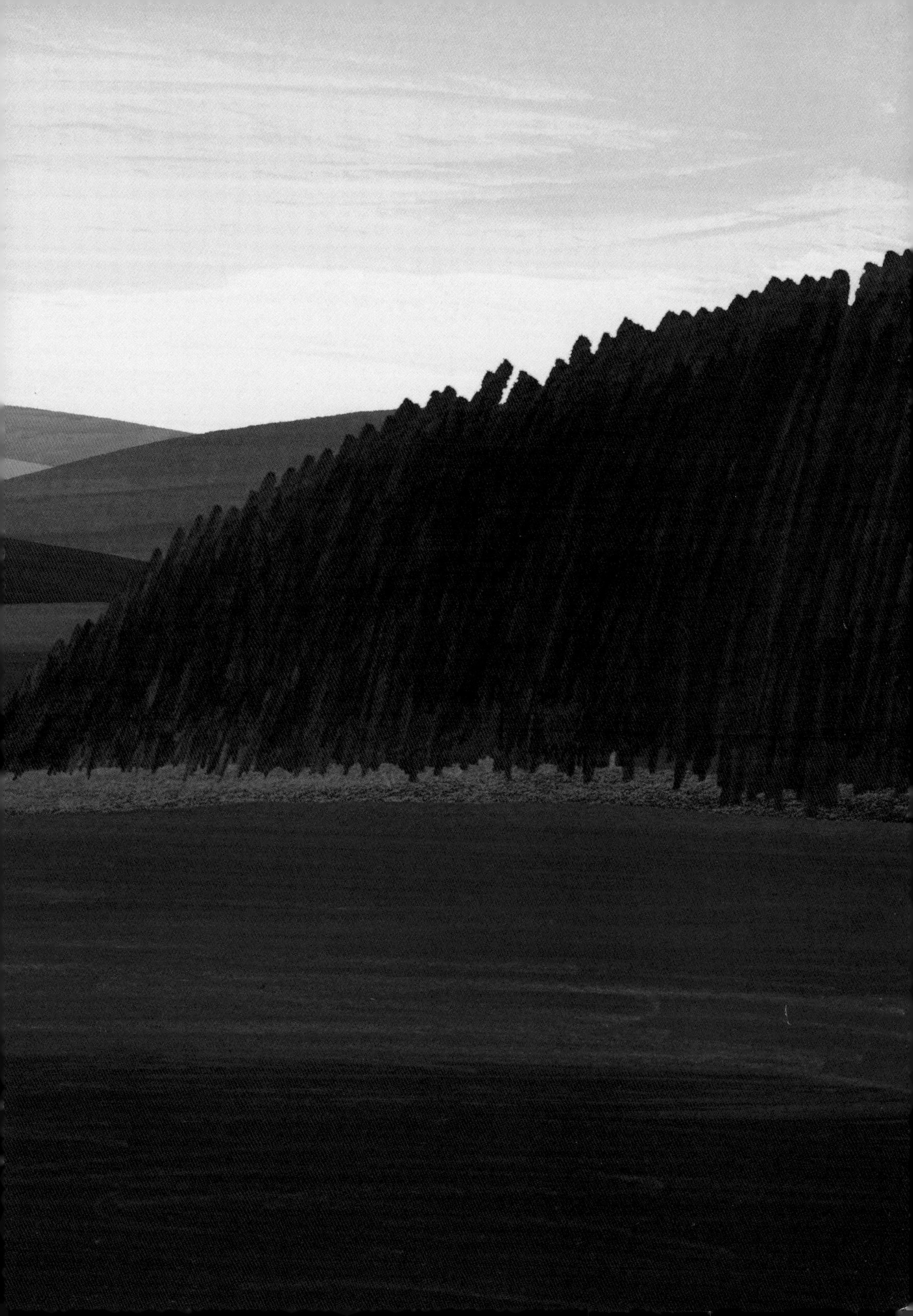

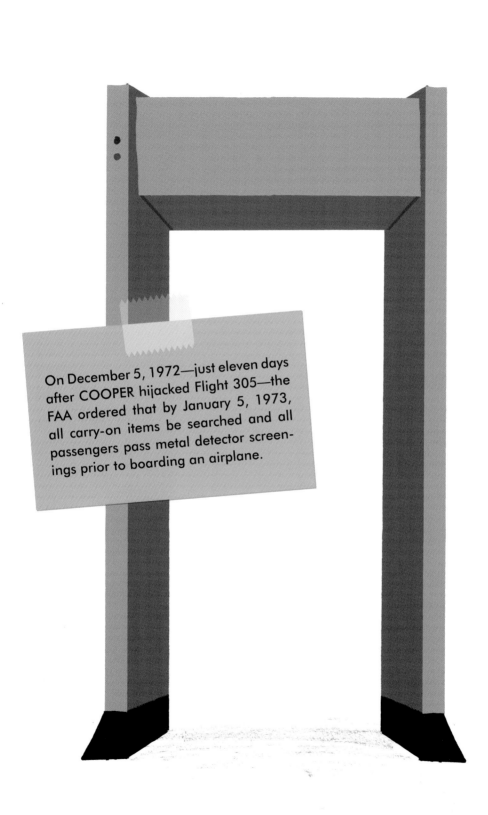

On December 5, 1972—just eleven days after COOPER hijacked Flight 305—the FAA ordered that by January 5, 1973, all carry-on items be searched and all passengers pass metal detector screenings prior to boarding an airplane.

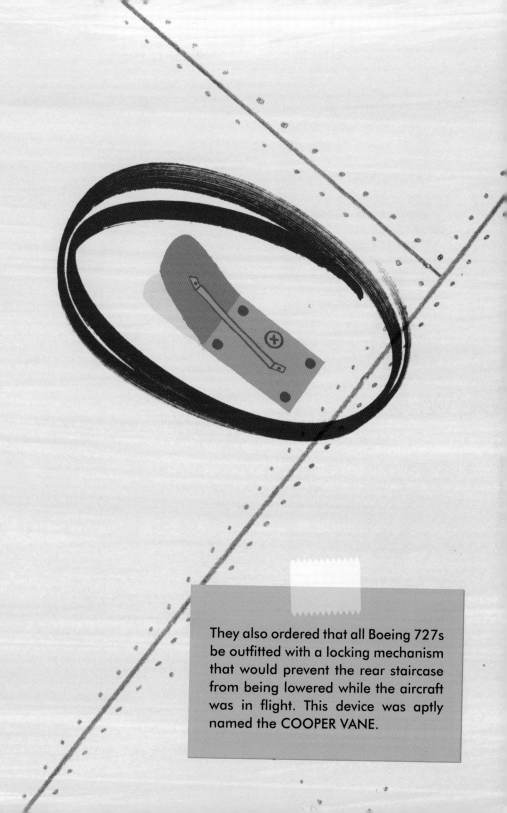

They also ordered that all Boeing 727s be outfitted with a locking mechanism that would prevent the rear staircase from being lowered while the aircraft was in flight. This device was aptly named the COOPER VANE.

PHOTOS FROM THE FILES

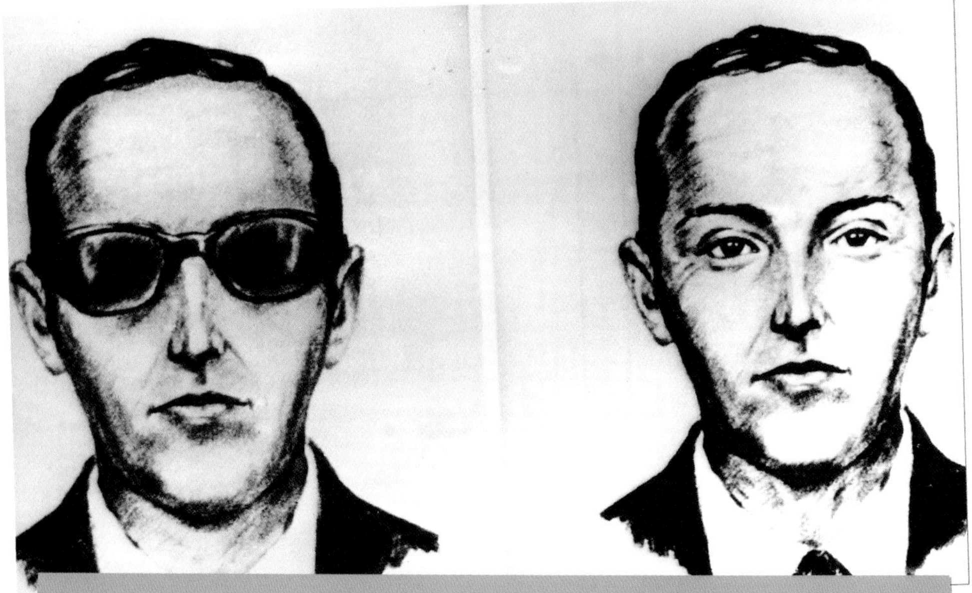

Composite sketches of D.B. COOPER based on eyewitness descriptions.

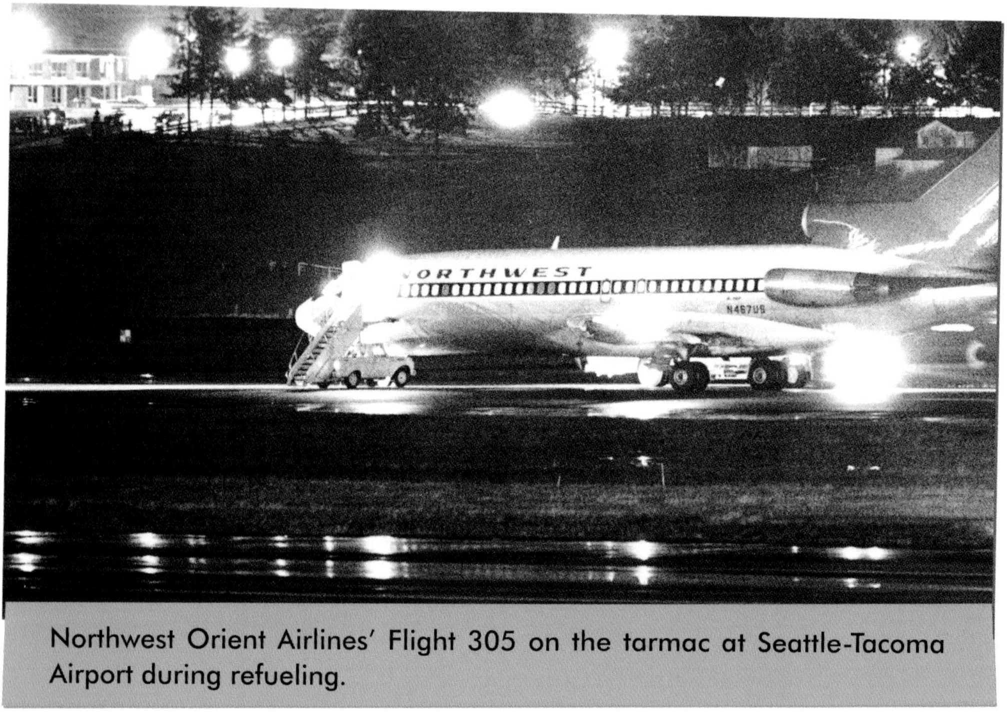

Northwest Orient Airlines' Flight 305 on the tarmac at Seattle-Tacoma Airport during refueling.

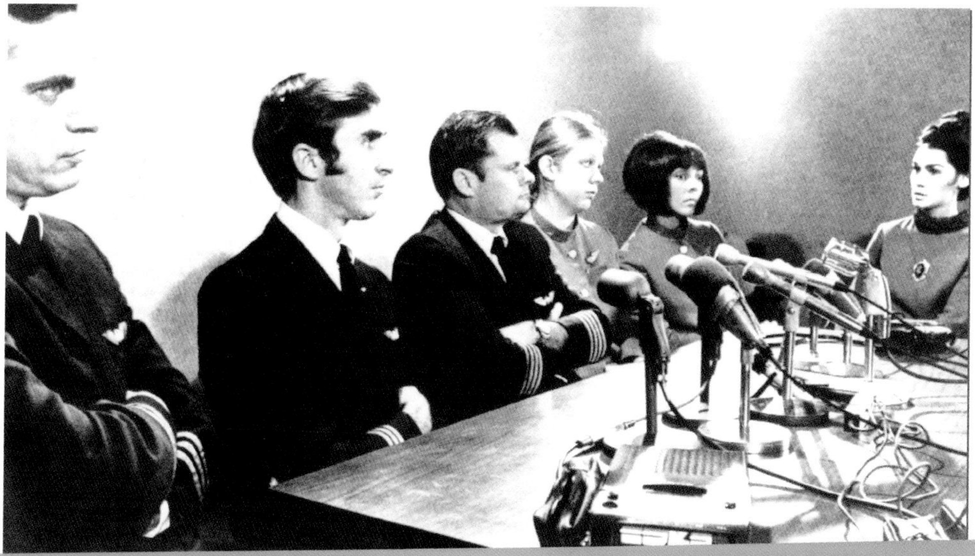

The flight crew, left to right: HAROLD E. ANDERSON, WILLIAM RATACZAK, Captain WILLIAM SCOTT, TINA MUCKLOW, FLORENCE SCHAFFNER, and ALICE HANCOCK.

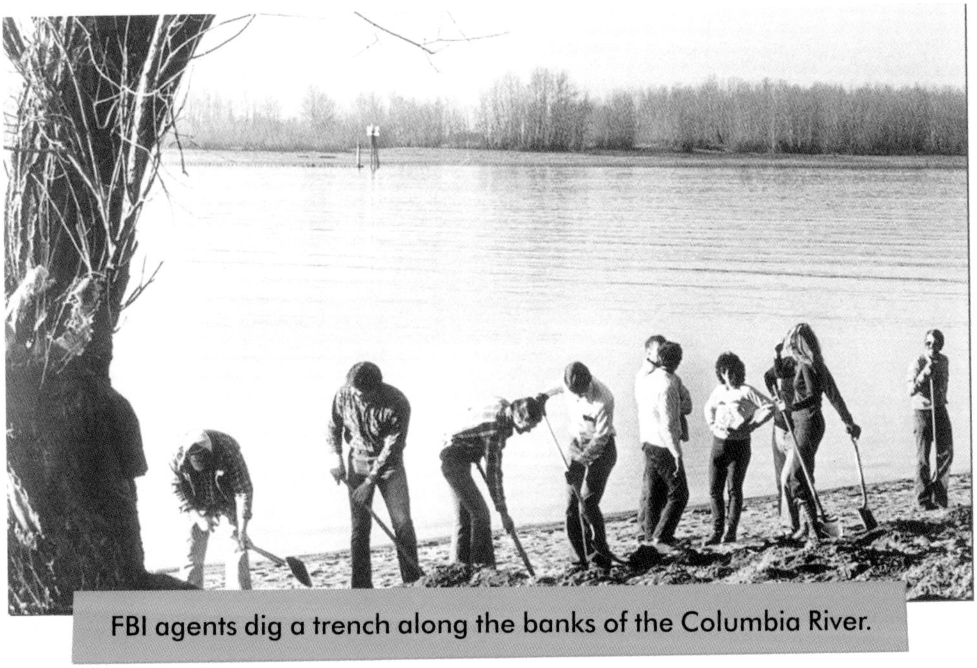

FBI agents dig a trench along the banks of the Columbia River.

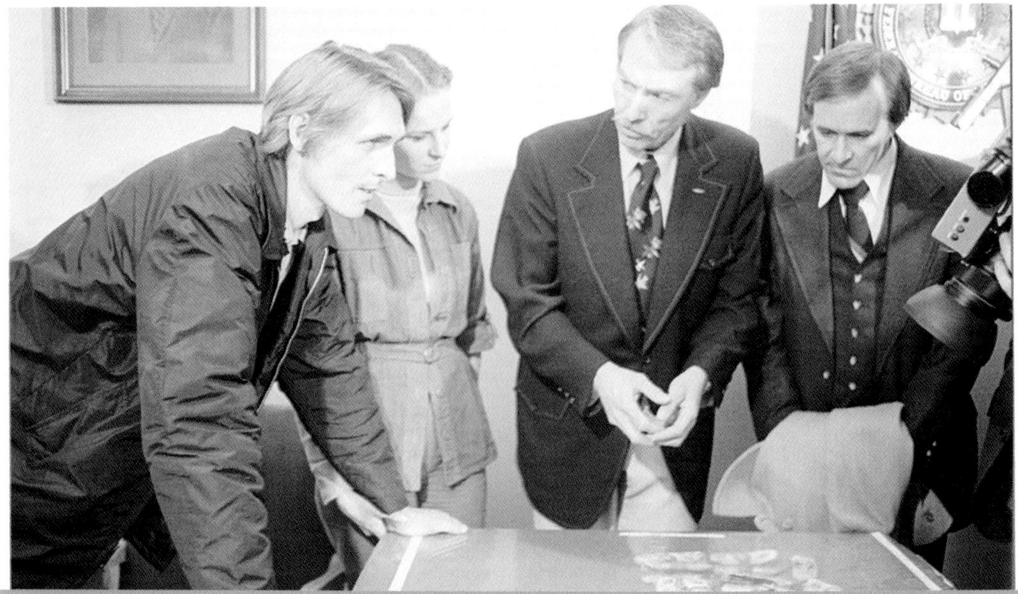

HAROLD and PATRICIA INGRAM, FBI special agent RALPH HIMMELSBACH, and a Northwest Orient Airlines representative examine the money found at Tena Bar.

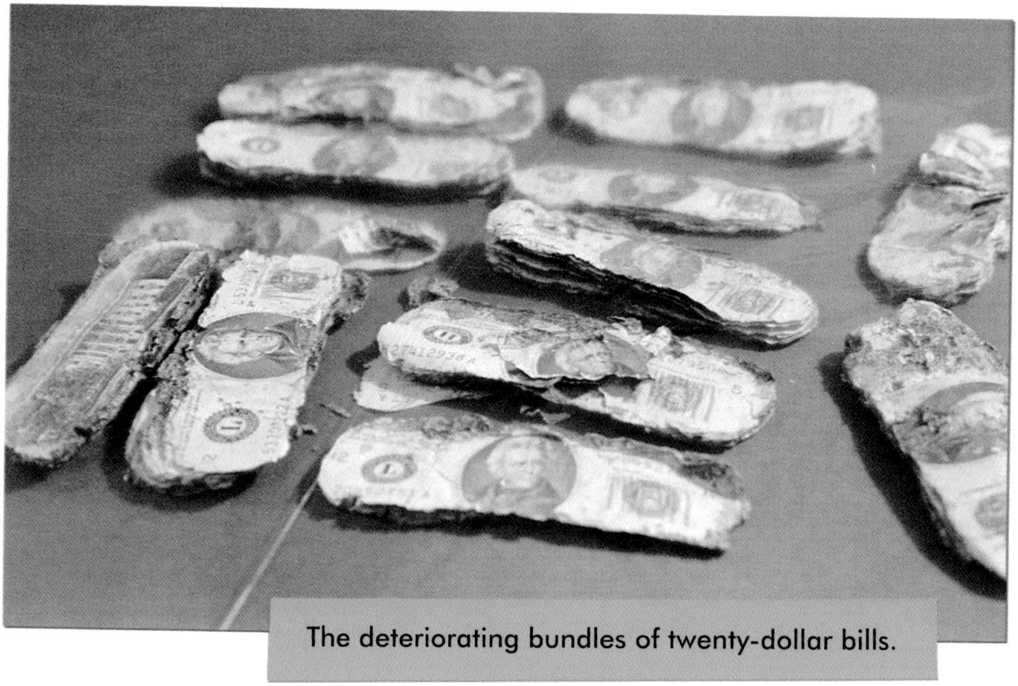

The deteriorating bundles of twenty-dollar bills.

WANTED

Race: White
Sex: Male
Age: Mid forties
Height: 5' 9" to 6'
Weight: 170 to 180 pounds
Build: Average to well built
Complexion: Olive, Latin appearance, medium smooth
Hair: Dark brown or black, normal style, parted on left, combed back, sideburns: low, ear level

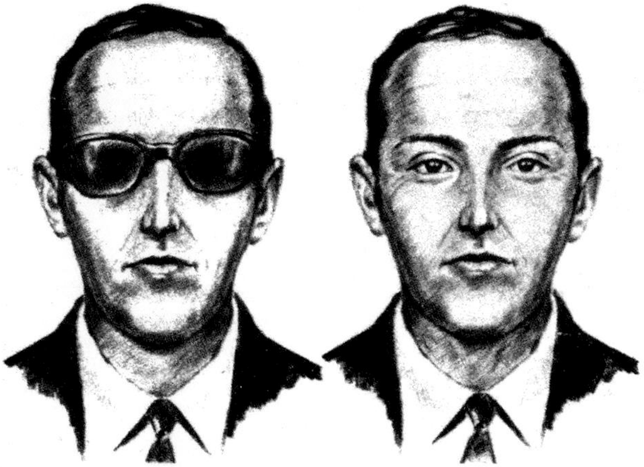

Eyes: Possibly brown, during latter part of flight put on dark wrap-around sunglasses with dark rims
Voice: Low, spoke intelligently, no particular accent, possibly from midwest section of the U.S.
Other: Heavy smoker of Raleigh filter tip cigarettes

The man who hijacked Northwest Airlines flight 305 on November 24, 1971 and extorted the airline out of $200,000. The identity of this individual remains unknown, but he purchased his ticket under the name Dan Cooper. He has subsequently become better known as

D. B. Cooper

$15,000

REWARD

If you have information regarding the identity or whereabouts of this individual, please contact the F.B.I. office in your area, the location and telephone number of which can be found in the front of your telephone directory.

This individul should be considered armed and dangerous. Under no circumstances should he be approached or capture attempted by anyone besides law enforcement officials.

To this day, the NORJAK (Northwest Hijacking) case remains the only unsolved skyjacking in US history.

On July 8, 2016, after forty-five frustrating years, the FBI officially suspended its active investigation into NORJAK in order to redirect resources to more pressing matters.

However, should new evidence surface, or if you or your family have any knowledge about the whereabouts or identity of the man they call D.B. COOPER, please contact your local FBI office.

SOURCES

All website URLs are accurate as of date of publication.

OVERVIEW OF THE CASE (INCLUDING FBI PRIMARY SOURCE MATERIALS):

"D.B. Cooper Hijacking." Famous Cases and Criminals. Federal Bureau of Investigation. Updated July 12, 2016. www.fbi.gov/history/famous-cases/db-cooper-hijacking.

Gray, Geoffrey. *Skyjack: The Hunt for D.B. Cooper.* New York: Broadway Books, 2012.

Himmelsbach, Ralph P. and Thomas K. Worcester. *Norjak: The Investigation of D.B. Cooper.* West Linn, OR: Norjak Project, 1986.

"In Search of D.B. Cooper: New Developments in the Unsolved Case." Archives. Federal Bureau of Investigation. March 17, 2009; updated July 12, 2016. https://archives.fbi.gov/archives/news/stories/2009/march/in-search-of-d.b.-cooper.

Swopes, Bryan R. "24 November 1971." This Day in Aviation: Important Dates in Aviation History. November 24, 2019. www.thisdayinaviation.com/24-november-1971/.

"The D.B. Cooper Project." True.Ink. https://true.ink/story/d-b-cooper-fbi-files-released/.

INFORMATION ABOUT PARACHUTES:

Smith, Bruce A. "DB Cooper Case Heats Up Again with Controversy Over Parachutes." *The Mountain News*, October 25, 2011. https://themountainnewswa.net/2011/10/25/db-cooper-case-heats-up-again-with-controversy-over-parachutes/.

AIRPORT SECURITY:

Lindsey, Robert. "Airports Start Thorough Screening of All Passengers." *New York Times*, January 6, 1973.

US TO CUBA HIJACKINGS:

"Havana-José Martí International Airport Profile." Database. Aviation Safety Network. Updated November 5, 2013. https://aviation-safety.net/database/airport/airport.php?id=HAV.

SUSPECT INFORMATION:

"Richard Floyd McCoy, Jr." Famous Cases and Criminals. Federal Bureau of Investigation. https://www.fbi.gov/history/famous-cases/richard-floyd-mccoy-jr.

MONEY FOUND AT TENA BAR:

Kaye, Tom. "The Hunt for D.B. Cooper." Citizen Sleuths. https://citizensleuths.com.

I ALSO OBTAINED SOME GREAT INFORMATION AND INSIGHT FROM AMATEUR WEBSITES DEDICATED TO THE CASE:

https://website.thedbcooperforum.com
https://web.archive.org/web/20181230233540/http://n467us.com/

COMING SOON:

JAILBREAK
AT ALCATRAZ

CASE No. 002_____